A PLACE CALLED
ARMAGEDDON
Letters from the Great War

Also edited by Michael Moynihan

People at War 1914–1918
People at War 1939–1945

A PLACE CALLED
ARMAGEDDON
Letters from the Great War

Edited with an introduction by
Michael Moynihan

*And he gathered them together into a place
called in the Hebrew tongue Armageddon*
Revelation of St John the Divine

DAVID & CHARLES

NEWTON ABBOT   LONDON
NORTH POMFRET (VT)   VANCOUVER

ISBN 0 7153 6959 8

Library of Congress Catalog Card Number 74-31965

Set in 11 on 13pt Baskerville and printed in
Great Britain by Latimer Trend & Company Ltd Plymouth
for David & Charles (Holdings) Limited
South Devon House   Newton Abbot   Devon

Published in the United States of America
by David & Charles Inc
North Pomfret Vermont 05053 USA

Published in Canada
by Douglas David & Charles Limited
132 Philip Avenue North Vancouver BC

Contents

		page
	List of Illustrations	7
	Foreword	9
	Introduction to Chapters 1 and 2	15
1	Guardsman Boorer—Traveller at Loos	19
2	'My Dearest Nell . . .'	36
3	Midshipman Drewry, VC	61
4	Gallipoli Survivor	77
5	Engineer on Horseback	104
6	Intrepid Birdman	134
7	Besieged in Kut	160
	Acknowledgements	191

List of Illustrations

PLATES *page*

Guardsman Boorer (*Imperial War Museum*)   49

Midshipman Drewry, VC (*Ralph Drewry*)   49

Captain Nightingale (*C. M. F. Coleman*)   49

Captain Martin (*Imperial War Museum*)   49

Guards Brigade prior to the Battle of Loos (*Imperial War Museum*)   50

Trooper R. C. Case (*Imperial War Museum*)   50

Cartoon by Bruce Bairnsfather (*Imperial War Museum*)   67

Gallipoli: landings from the *River Clyde* (*Imperial War Museum*)   68

Kut: surgeons operating (*Imperial War Museum*)   68

MAPS

The landings at Gallipoli   78

Mesopotamia, showing the position of Kut   161

Foreword

Rank upon rank of box-files, stacked along steel shelves in a spacious strong-room at the Imperial War Museum in London, contain a record of the two world wars unparalleled anywhere in the world—the diaries, letters, journals and miscellaneous papers of many hundreds of the men and women who took part in them. From a once-famous brass-hat's voluminous correspondence to a private's barely legible diary jottings in a field note-book, they provide a unique hunting ground for the military historian.

For the casual reader most of the semi-official documents bequeathed to posterity by high-ranking officers would prove heavy going. But in recent years the museum has cast its net wider. A Department of Documents has been scouring the country for any written records of the two wars, however seemingly trivial. Obituary columns have been combed for the names of veterans who may have had diaries or bundles of letters tucked away in an attic trunk or deed-box, appeals have been published in the press, second-hand bookshops alerted, war veteran associations consulted. The search has been particularly urgent among the rapidly dwindling numbers of World War I survivors, the youngest now in their seventies.

The haul has already been a rich one, much of it consisting of the diaries and letters of ordinary men and women who had no preconception that their private jottings would one day be valued additions to national archives. It is from among these people that the seven collections of letters, from which this book has been compiled, have been selected.

This book is in the nature of a companion volume to two similar collections, published under the title *People at War*, which were based on diaries and journals from the two world wars. *The Sunday Times* had invited readers to send in their war stories, and it was from the best of these and from the best of the Imperial War Museum's recent acquisitions that the books were compiled. Public interest in the museum's search for documents was further aroused by the publication in *The Sunday Times* of two long extracts from *People at War 1914–1918*, and it is because this resulted in a number of varied war records being sent to the museum (including some of the letters used here) that I again had the absorbing task of shaping a book from the grass-root experiences of war.

Switching from diaries and journals to letters was to see war in a new, more piercing light. Diaries (unless mere records of events) may be more revealing of a man's innermost thoughts, but they are by their nature self-conscious exercises, usually showing the writer to the best advantage and often written with the possibility of eventual publication in mind. Journals written in retrospect inevitably concentrate on the most memorable happenings, skirting over those long periods of routine activity and boredom which took up so much of the time even of the soldier at the Front. To see a man whole, as he was seen and known by those closest to him, there is nothing more revealing than the letters he wrote home. As we follow his handwriting down the page, it is like looking over a shoulder. And from what he writes we may see him, not in isolation, but closely linked to family and friends rooted in his past.

The seven very different individuals portrayed experienced war in all its aspects—hellish and elating, degrading and ennobling, tragic and comic. Two of the letter-writers are still alive, and in talking to them it is apparent how many of these aspects are juxtaposed in their memories of the Great War, still hauntingly close after the lapse of over half a century. Relatives of the others, three of whom lost their lives in the war, have been consulted where possible. The son and daughter of Guardsman Boorer could speak only from hearsay—they had been too young to remember their father when he was killed by a sniper's bullet on the Western Front. The younger brother of Midshipman Drewry, a national hero when he was awarded the VC at Gallipoli, still mourns his death. A niece of Captain Nightingale, whose descriptions of the fighting at Gallipoli are among the most remarkable to have come to light, had only once met her uncle, decorated for valour, who took his own life twenty years later. The unpredictability of human nature pervades those brave and bouyant letters from one of the war's bloodiest battlefields.

As human documents these letters have a timeless appeal, but in reading some of them one needs to be aware of the emotional climate of the period, in many respects quite alien to that which permeated the last war. As a war correspondent, who saw something of the fighting in three theatres of war, I can recall few instances of the bloodthirsty attitude to the enemy evinced in some of these letters. There is Captain Nightingale writing of the savage fighting at Gallipoli—'All the streams were simply running blood and the heaps of dead were a grand sight.' There is Captain Case's reference to the roars of laughter from a group of young volunteers awaiting active service that greeted the gruesome stories told by an officer just back from the front in 1916: like the one of the sapper chasing a burly German who had joined up with a bunch of hastily retreating Tommies and who 'with a mighty effort sliced off the Hun's pate with a single blow of his shovel'. There is Lieutenant Kirkpatrick, of the RFC, describing the pilot of a German plane shot down over the Allied lines as 'done to a frazzle', writing to his family 'I know you all like meaty details'—and proceeding to give them.

From all accounts hatred of the Hun was far more prevalent on the Home Front than in the trenches, with jingoistic newspapers spreading atrocity stories, cartoonists depicting the Kaiser in more fiendish forms than even Hitler was to attain, patriotism exalted into a religion, crowds gathering to gloat over the charred remains of zeppelins. The civilian soldier would have absorbed much of this hysteria by the time he reached the front, there to discover that it had little relevance to the realities of trench warfare. In this dehumanised war of attrition, this indiscriminate slaughter by shells, bullets, gas, it was difficult not to regard the enemy, mostly invisible in his trenches the other side of no man's land but enduring the same squalour of mud, rats and lice, as a fellow-victim. Such warfare was almost impossible to communicate to the patriots at home.

Case, who had enlisted in the Yeomanry confident that war would prove a 'jolly good sporting show', attempts to dispel the illusions in a number of his letters: 'The very thought of this warfare makes one sick and disgusted,' he writes from the trenches near Arras. Even Nightingale, a regular army officer who displays a positive zest for battle in some of his earlier letters, reflects, from the temporary sanctum of a hospital ship: 'I am just beginning to feel again that life is worth living when you once get away from nasty things like bullets and stray limbs and decomposed corpses.'

In talking to veterans of the Great War like Case and Kirkpatrick, it becomes apparent how difficult it is for later generations to appreciate what to them were the normal reactions of the fighting man. Today, at the age of eighty-one, Case can vividly recall that evening in an English camp when he 'rocked with laughter' at those chilling tales from the front. 'It was the first time we had personal contact with anyone who had been at the front and we novices listened entranced. Strange as it may seem reading them today in cold blood, they seemed to us then to be immensely entertaining and amusing. It all seemed part of the game at that time, and you must remember that to us violence was a virtue.'

In the letters that follow there is far more of human warmth, of cheerful endurance and optimism, of the comforting trivia that exercise the mind even in the direst circumstance, than of the darker side of war. But one is always aware of the blood-bath in progress, the spectacle (as Case put it) of 'the most cultivated nations upon earth (as we smugly imagine ourselves) waging the dirtiest and most unsporting warfare that could possibly be imagined'. And at a time when doom is being cried from so many quarters, it may be salutary to count our blessings, looking back to a time in living memory when 15 million men were killed in battle or died of their wounds in a climate of hatred where violence was seen as a virtue and man's inhumanity to man had become an accepted way of life.

Introduction to Chapters 1 and 2

Among all the first-hand accounts of the Great War, one voice has been conspicuously absent: the voice of the Tommy. For the most part it is through the eyes of the young officer that we form our impressions of what life was like at the front. The rank and file who bore the brunt of the hazards and privations—the Poor Bloody Infantry—remain shadowy figures. Even in the detailed accounts of battles in official regimental histories they are very rarely mentioned by name. We can glimpse them as the camera froze them for an instant, on the march, huddled in trenches, faces gaunt or grinning under their steel helmets, or in flickering newsreels jerking over the top into no man's land. We can warm to them in the guise of Bruce Bairnsfather's Old Bill, or the Tommy of *Punch* cartoons—salty, grizzling, imperturbable characters, soldiering on whatever the odds. We can weep for them in rage and pity as Wilfred Owen did, pawns in a war of attrition, cattle driven to the slaughter. But they remain types rather than recognisable human beings.

In recent years there has been a spate of retrospective journals written in retirement by other rank war veterans, and the few published do give a fresh focus to the war as the majority of fighting men experienced it. But inevitably it is a picture blurred and distorted by time. Only in letters written at the front to wives, parents and friends at home could one be sure of an authentic insight into their true feelings. And the fact that very few of these have come to light leaves a significant gap in our understanding of the war.

The editor of a recent war anthology suggested that such letters would be of little interest in that most of the rank and file of the Great War were ill-educated, semi-literate and unable to express themselves in writing. There are, indeed, allusions to the laboured style and mundane content of soldiers' letters in the diaries and letters of junior officers, whose duty it was to censor their men's mail. But to dismiss as irrelevant that vast bulk of letters, scribbled in dugout, tent or billet, that kept hope alive in so many homes throughout Britain is altogether too sweeping and arbitrary a judgement.

The two collections of letters that follow—written to their wives by a Grenadier Guardsman and a Royal Marines sergeant—have only recently come into the possession of the Imperial War Museum, where they are prized as a rarity. Both men were killed in action and the fact that they had been preserved over the years by their widows suggests that others like them may still be in existence, most likely to be thrown away as valueless when there is no one left alive to treasure them. The Marine's bulky collection of letters was found on a rubbish dump.

The marked difference in style and content between the two collections underlines the fallacy of generalisation. Guardsman Boorer had a good education, was a commercial traveller when he enlisted and writes briskly, with an eye to what is going on around him. Sergeant Fielder, a regular for some years before the war, writes with laboured earnestness or jocularity, showing an obsessive concern for the wife and small son he has left behind, and rarely referring to his own doings. The most noticeable similarity is the brief, almost off-hand way in which they allude to two of the war's bloodiest engagements in which they took part—Boorer in the Battle of Loos, Fielder in the fighting after the first landings in Gallipoli.

Censorship apart, concern for their wives is an obvious reason for this reticence—'I don't know whether I'm right in telling you this, because you worry so,' writes Fielder in a letter describing the savagery of trench warfare. But it could also indicate a subconscious defence mechanism, turning a blind eye on the horrors in order to keep going. War veterans have revealed how long-buried memories surfaced long after the war in nightmares, how they had never spoken of their grimmest experiences even to their wives and that the urge to write a journal was largely to exorcise obsessive memories.

One may now regret that there is not more in these letters about the actual fighting. But read merely as human documents, showing ordinary men facing up to extraordinary events, preoccupied with the trivia of daily existence, sustained above all by the letters and lovingly prepared parcels from the home they yearned for, they bring us a little closer to the reality of their experience.

1   Guardsman Boorer—Traveller at Loos

In army records the relevant facts about Private Herbert G. Boorer are briefly stated. Born Lewisham, enlisted in Grenadier Guards on 2 September 1914, aged 26 years 350 days. Five feet 11 inches, hazel eyes, brown hair. Mole right of right nipple. Roman Catholic. Wife Ann Catherine, 44 Muirkirk Road, Catford, SE6. Children Kathleen Mary, Francis, John. Trade traveller. No 18036, Private Machine Gun Section 4th Battalion Grenadier Guards, BEF. Arrived France 15 August 1915, killed by sniper 4 December.

The twelve letters he wrote to his wife from France reveal him as physically tough and mentally resilient. He takes in his stride the meagre rations, the gruelling forced marches in full kit ('we lose pounds in weight I reckon'), sleeping on the floors of stables and cowsheds, the tormenting lice, the heat, mud and freezing cold. He refers almost nonchalantly to the hazards and horrors of the battlefield—advancing in the open at Loos 'under terrific shellfire', lying on corpses in a recently bombarded German trench, the effects of a gas attack. In a letter of condolence to his widow, his section officer wrote: 'He is a great loss to me as he was a splendid soldier and had a splendid character.'

Boorer's letters were presented to the Imperial War Museum by his surviving son, John, after he had read in *The Sunday Times* of their search for first-hand war records. He had been unaware of their existence until recently when he happened to mention to his sister, Mrs Kathleen Goddard, that he was engaged in tracing the history of the Boorer family. Their mother had lived with her and the deed box in which she had kept the letters had passed into her possession after her death in 1941.

'I had known about them but somehow could not bring myself to read them,' says Mrs Goddard. 'We were all too young to have any recollection of our father, but even as a child I remember being terribly upset during the two minutes' silence on Armistice Day. Even now I feel it would be too distressing to brood over them.'

To John Boorer, who was just over two years old when his father was killed (his sister was four) the letters were a revelation. 'I remember as a child the enlarged studio photograph of my father in Guard's uniform that used to hang on the sitting-room wall, but he was always a shadowy figure to me. He came alive when I read these letters and I was deeply moved. I was very struck by their quality and it was extraordinary how they filled in the gaps when I looked up the official history of the Guards at the dates of the letters. They put life into that dry account.'

From what they had learned as children about their father, Mr Boorer and Mrs Goddard were able to provide some background facts. Son of a master carpenter at Drury Lane Theatre (where he constructed the first revolving stage), Herbert Boorer was educated at Haberdashers' Aske's School in London and was doing well as a commercial traveller (in chocolates) when he enlisted. He had been a keen sportsman and had the required physique, as well as height, for the Brigade of Guards.

His wife was a devout Catholic, of Irish stock, and his own

conversion to Catholicism shortly before their marriage in 1910 was not well received by his own Protestant family. But by the war it had become a united family circle. The letters have many references to parcels from home to which both families contributed.

A parcel from home was always a red-letter day in a Tommy's spartan existence at the front. The two letters from Mrs Boorer to her husband which have survived are almost entirely concerned with items sent or asked for. Food and clothes apart, Boorer appreciated the occasional bottle of 'medicine', but the recurring request is for cigarettes. 'The cigarettes came just in time as I smoked my last in the trenches,' he writes in one letter, and one is suddenly aware of how much the habits of civilian life clung. To Boorer, as to any non-regular soldier, the war was only tolerable because seen as an interlude to normal life. And to his widow, brooding over these letters, there must have been an unbearable poignancy in the last sentences he wrote, six days before his death: 'Plenty of love when it can find outward expression. Here's to the time when Old Bill chucks his mitt in.'

The summer of 1915 had been relatively quiet on the Western Front, and for Boorer the first few weeks in France until the Battle of Loos followed much the same routine as in England, route marches, field days, machine-gun practice. His first four letters home are undated.

'Dear Kit, I have had a champion ride of 20 hours in a cattle-truck since I wrote that card. Thirty-two of us in one truck. The weather here is splendid. Just a little too hot perhaps when you are carrying full kit. Are now in billets. They feed us on corned beef and dog biscuits. These biscuits are all right, although a trifle hard. Nothing doing today. The French shops in small places are very funny, you can hardly tell they are shops. There are usually about 10 cafés to one other shop.

I think there will be a shortage of matches soon as they are dear here, so always send some when sending cigarettes. French cigarettes are not up to much. The MG section is in a large place over the motor garage attached to a large house. The rest of the Battalion are scattered round in different places. There does not seem much to say so au revoir. Love to yourself and kiddies, Bert.'

'. . . We had a nice wet day yesterday, when we did about 16 miles. We came back to our billets last Saturday. The books are all right but one at a time is sufficient as there is difficulty in looking after them, as we have to carry all our kit with us. Will send you an occasional pair of socks, as I am no hand at mending them. The BDV tobacco is the best, I could do with some more and cigarettes. I should think 50 cigarettes and 2oz tobacco would do per week, together with a few that we get issued sometimes. I have bought another pipe. Have had 5 francs pay up to now, about 4/2. I have not any news much, so ta ta for the present . . . Have had head cropped, front as well. Look frightfully smart.'

'. . . The MG section is staying in a small camp outside a convent, which is being used as a MG school, about 5 miles away from the Battalion. It is practically the same as we have already learned with just a few new ideas. It is mainly for a new section just starting. We are in just the same position here as when in England, we do not know what is coming off. We can hear the boom of the big guns in the distance, especially in the early morning and evening when things are quiet. There are also bags of aeroplanes. We are not allowed to go into the nearest town, but have to stick to the country. Not much grub here. Shall be glad to get back to the billet.

'Have had an issue of cigarettes and tobacco but the cigarettes have all gone. French ones are black and much too strong for us. Beer here is 1d a pint, but you cannot get drunk on it. I got in that happy state however just before we left Marlow, and met the ground on quite a number of occasions. Anyway I had to resort to my knee-caps the following day. Taking things all round, it is pretty cushy out here so far, but hardly exciting enough. Do not forget to keep the cigarettes going. Hope you are all going strong . . .

'. . . We are all more or less 'cooty' [lousy] but not being particular sort of chaps we have a grand raid on them now and then and let it go at that. Some of the boys have got various kinds of powder, and as I expect they will get worse you might send along anything that is reckoned good. Have not been to confession yet. Have not opened Dad's tin of matches as Mum sent me some, also candles and soap. Have not been in trenches yet, and do not know when I shall go. There is a heavy bombardment going on within hearing. There are many large crucifixes and statues about the countryside. Am well and in good form as we do plenty of hard marching every day . . .

'. . . Am doing guards at last, on our billet. Of course there are no blankets out here, just our overcoats and consequently trousers are on for the duration of the war. When on guard but not on sentry, we sleep on bricks, and in the ordinary way we have a splendidly level floor, with not even a suspicion of a hole to put a hip into, but of course we have been trained to appreciate these things. Have "found" a dog, which is a bitch, and call it Nutmeg, to fit in with some initials already on the collar. There is really nothing doing here other than the ordinary training. I believe there is another big divisional field day tomorrow. More hard work for me having to carry the gun. We are not allowed to wander far afield. All farms and cultivated ground round here . . .

'. . . We have another billet at a farm. We live in a stable, and have some straw, but space is somewhat limited. Weather is still good, but it gets rather cold at night. In the daytime we lose pounds in weight I reckon. Managed to win 3 francs at Pontoon last night before they stopped us. The dog has done a nip. Followed some other mob I expect . . . There might be something doing for me in a week or two. Then again there

23

might not. Much love to all, yourself and kiddies. We'll make
it all up when we see each other again, eh.'

The 'something doing' was to be the Battle of Loos, 25–7
September, one of the bloodiest brief engagements of the war, in
which there were nearly 50,000 British and 20,000 German
casualties. The assault, in which seven British divisions were
engaged, was preceded by a four-day artillery bombardment of
the mining village of Loos and the grey surrounding area of pit-
heads and slagheaps, and the 'British victory' to which Boorer
refers in his next letter indicates the initial breakthrough by
the Scottish 15th Division which carried them some miles
beyond Loos. Through lack of support, however, they were
forced to retire, and by the time the newly created Guards
Division, held in reserve with two other divisions, went into
action the following day the Germans had sealed off the salient
and were ready for them.

Boorer's battalion formed part of the 3rd Guards Brigade,
whose demeanour as they went into battle that Sunday morning, 26 September, has passed into military legend. The
official history of the Grenadier Guards describes how, as they
reached the top of a ridge and advanced in artillery formation in
full view of the Germans, 'perfect order was maintained in
spite of the shells, which burst all round, and there was not a
man out of his place. Nothing more splendid has ever been
recorded in the annals of the Guards than the manner in which
every battalion in the Brigade faced this trying ordeal.' A
general is quoted as having described it as 'one of the most
splendid and inspiring sights I have ever seen'.

In her deed box alongside her husband's letters Mrs Boorer
kept a faded cutting from the *Daily Chronicle* in which their
special correspondent, Philip Gibbs, described the battle. She
would have known, from what her husband later wrote, that a
machine-gun section did not take part in the initial wave of an
assault, but even so must have found it hard to equate his off-
hand account with the high-flown language of the despatch—

'safeguarding the honour of a famous name', 'such supreme contempt for death that even the enemy must have been moved to admiration'.

The last undated letter was evidently written the day before Boorer went into action for the first time, after a series of forced marches to the battle area. There is then a week's gap before his all-too-brief reference to the battle.

'We have been on the move since Wednesday, marching mostly in the darkness to billets in stables each day. Have just heard of British victory in front of us, trenches taken and Germans gassed. We stuck to the by-roads and small villages. These places seem very poor. The flashes of the guns look like lightning at night. The bombardment has been continuous for days until this morning when we broke through and the news came through as I have said. Am going on all right, got three hours in the rain the other night, but it is practically the first we have had, and I can always get along better in the wet and mud myself. Hope you are all fit there. You have seen worse than I have, when you saw the Zeppelin . . . Won another 10 francs at Pontoon yesterday.'

'*2 October*. Have had a cut at them this time. Was in action from Monday last until early Thursday morning. Have got through all right, and am having a few days' rest before having another go. We advanced through the open under terrific shell fire. I was in the first-line trench for thirty hours in the pouring rain, smothered from head to foot with mud. One of our limbers got smashed up, and my kit has gone west. I think I prefer the trench to a bit further back where the Jack Johnsons fall. I was nearly lifted off the ground several times by them, and am not exactly in love with them. I do not mind the bullets and shrapnel so much.

'The Battalion had a pretty rough time, but a lot of ground has been gained near here during the last week or so. I cannot tell you all about it, but it is something you cannot realise until you get in it. The German snipers are pretty hot. Our MG section only lost two, and we came off very well compared with the companies. Your parcel was waiting when I got back. I suggest that you send quite small ones in future, as we shall be on the move a lot probably and it will be quite impossible to carry a big one. Have lost my cap also. Could do with some paper and envelopes. Am back in a village now just behind our artillery in a stable. The cigarettes came just in time as I smoked my last in the trenches. A miss is as good as a mile so they say, so am carrying on about the same as ever . . . Do not worry. Am going strong.'

'*8 October.* I suppose you have got my first letter about the fight now. I expect you have read about it in the paper. The second time I was in a different place, my particular gun was supporting the 1st Battalion guns as they have had a lot of casualties. I am in a ruined house now. Our guns are going off just outside, and German Jack Johnsons are falling round about it now and again just to keep things lively. One has just dropped across the road as I write this. I have been missed scores of times by bullets and stray bits of shrapnel during the last week, and have got quite used to it. We have periods of desperate work carting guns and kit about, on very little to eat and nothing much to drink when in the trenches or else having a pot at them or waiting patiently for things to happen. I get very cold at night here. Sleep seems to be a thing of the past, but we do not care a ——. Do not ask me to write to anyone as I would rather go into the trenches again than write letters. You might pass any news on. The sixth JJ has just dropped amongst this bunch of ruined houses since I mentioned the last one. I do not think anyone was hurt though . . . Tell the kiddies we'll all have a holiday when I come back. Stick it Kit till then.'

'*20 October.* I think I had better deal with your questions first. You can send the gloves as I have been nearly frozen stiff the last five days. I have a stocking cap, or rather I have borrowed one. Will let you know if I have to give it back. The tin of matches I had on me in my haversack when I lost my pack and kit on the limber and have still a few left.

'No ground has been lost by the Guards. On the contrary we have been doing nothing else but attacking and taking ground since we started. It was us that started the ball the first time in action and took Hill 70 and Loos . . . Machine-guns cannot charge with the infantry, as of course they cannot get along quick enough. They give covering fire from the original position, and follow up immediately the infantry are in, to hold the new position against counter attack when the troops are exhausted and the position is not at all secure . . . I have not seen any churches, only ruined ones, or priests, and Sundays seem to be the particular day all parties prefer to kick up merry hell . . .

'Well we have been in the front line again from last Thursday until yesterday evening. I think I had about five hours sleep in five days and was pretty well done up when I arrived here just behind the trenches, but feel fine this morning after a feed and good sleep. We looked very pretty, I quite admired myself, I imagine I looked like a Californian gold miner you read about. Five days' beard, no wash. But instead covered with dirt all over face, inside shirt, where it goes down the neck clothes one cake of it. Stocking cap on, and one of those khaki handkerchiefs round neck.

'The strain is finding out the boys' weak spots. Half the section have gone sick with various complaints. Also we had three gassed going in, and one wounded. I suppose the gassed ones did not get the smoked helmet on quick enough. I got a breath or two, but it did not affect me. And when I got my helmet on it was worse than the gas. You have to breathe through thick shirting saturated with chemicals, which you put over the head and tuck into your shirt and button round, with a little transparent stuff to look through, which puzzles you to do, as it gets misty from your breath. There must be something to protect the eyes as it affects them first.

'We are having it thick here, as there is no peace for a

minute, being nearly all attacking. There was a bombing attack by the brigade bombers who took part of the German trench. My particular gun had to go and hold it a few minutes afterwards, although it was in the Scots Guards part of the trenches. It was a dead end, with nothing but a barricade between us and the Germans. Dead men hanging over the trenches, blown almost inside out. Had to work, and lay on a few covered with a few inches of dirt in the bottom of the trench. More were put into niches in the sides, with bayonets stuck in to keep them falling out. They are calling for letters at once so must finish or it will not go . . . PTO. We should have been in for it if they had crawled up and bombed us in the night but we kept putting bursts over the barricade, and they did not do so. We were sniped at from all angles however. There was just six of us in this bit, on our own, so you can guess sleep was hardly safe. We brought six out so all's well that ends well.'

'*29 October*. I hope you have sent off more cigarettes by now. Send 100 a week. The scarf and helmet will come in handy. Thank your Dad, also my Dad, Mum and Grandma when you see them. Went in the first line again for 3 days and now have come back about 10 miles for a fortnight rest. We have not done so bad, either being in, or first reserve since we started. Had rain this time and as I said before bad weather is worse than the Germans in the trenches. Had a lot of hard work, but nothing wildly exciting. Have got a new cap, but had to go into the trenches without a shirt on, as I had worn the only one I possessed until you could not tell which was shirt and which was lice. I am still without and look like remaining so. You might send a box of Harrison's Pomade as they say it is good, and I am tearing myself to shreds. We are now in the usual cowshed, with cows and pigs on either side. Some of the boys have the cheek to tell me I am looking well on this kind of thing.'

'*7 November*. Received your two parcels alright. They were

both smashed but I do not think there was anything missing. Have managed to get a shirt so am well off with two now. Tell Dad the medicine is "bon". What Jim says about the Battalion refers to the Division. We are always on the spot where things are moving and I have never been in the same spot twice, in fact I usually have to shift two or three times when I am in. I expect we shall be going up again next week early. Last time in, the water was over our boot tops, and as we have had a lot of rain since I expect the trenches are in a lovely state. It is pretty cold here now. Feet are the worst, our boots are always more or less wet through . . . You might put a couple of shillings in the cigarettes in the next parcel, as I have only 2d and do not know when we shall be paid again, and it is handy to buy a bit of extra bread etc. Took one of our chaps away ill on a stretcher the other day, I think he is in England now. We have another slightly loopy . . .'

The last letter Mrs Boorer was to receive from her husband was written on the backs of the last two she had sent to him. How typical they are of others she had written it is impossible to guess, but their preoccupation with the contents of parcels, without mention of her husband's ordeals, seems strange at first sight. It could be that she felt a helplessness to do more than fuss over his needs, to reassure him that life was going on as usual at home. Each item in a parcel was tangible evidence of loving concern, and it could be that a jealous mention of the quality of somebody else's home-made cake brought a warmer reflection of home to the trenches than any amount of words.

'(?) *November*. It is a long while now since you wrote, but I suppose you are alright, I heard you had written to your Mum last Monday. How were Dorothy's *famous* cakes, were they better than mine, I have heard such a lot of charving about them it made me wonder if they were so very nice. I have sent another parcel off last Friday and did not put any cigarettes in because I knew your Dad was sending you a lot, let me know before you run short of them, and my Dad contributed the pineapple tin, I have to let you know who sends things. *I* contributed the rest. Did you get Minnie's cigarettes she sent you, she keeps asking me if I know. Let me know how you liked the tin of tomatoes and also the sauce because I do not want to send things that you do not want. Dad heard me speaking about the mice eating the things and he says he can send you a fancy tin box with a handle and lock and key to keep your biscuits and such things locked up if you will let me know.'

'*24 November*. I got your long-delayed letter and I am very sorry about your kit, did somebody steal it or was it sent back. I suppose you have lost the tin match box now and was it the pair of mits Grandma sent you, you are unfortunate. I have sent a parcel today instead of Friday (that is the 2nd since the last one you mentioned) and put some "medicine" in and Dorothy made the sponge and put the jam separate to spread over it and she also sent the box of sweets and Ida Jarratt, a cousin I believe, made the mittens for you and your "Aunt Amy" that lived in Malpas Road sent a tin of cigarettes, and I have also put in two soup packets, let me know how you get on with them.

'We are just starting on the Christmas puddings, I took the three kiddies to the Cave at Cheismans and they all had a toy. I saw young Bobbie Leroche yesterday, you know he was supposed to be seriously wounded at the "Dardanelles", he was not wounded nearly as much as made out. I put some shaving soap in as well, I thought you might like it. How will you manage about a shirt, I have not got any more flannel ones, I have got the fellow undervest to the one I sent you. Let me know if you want it and I shall buy a flannel shirt.

'Well darling I think this is all now, and I am pleased that the children seem to be picking up again. Look after yourself and come back soon, with much love Kit. The babies send love and kisses to Dadda and Kittie says she is going to cuddle you when you come home wounded.'

Boorer's last letter is dated 28 November.

'At last I have a Sunday out of the trenches. We have come back for a few days and are in the usual barn. We have also had a little snow and it has been freezing hard for the last week. It is a bit of a devil when you cannot get your boots on in the morning because they are frozen stiff, and they have been lying beside your head all night. You can guess the condition of your feet when you eventually do get them on. Have been too cold to write till now, when I have got into a pub with 1½d. You had better send some money at the double as I have only been paid 5 francs (about 3/8 English!) in about 5 weeks.

'Have had your two letters and parcels also letters from your brothers. Have got a leather waistcoat but am not allowed to wear it except in the trenches. The apples were good. You can send a bottle of Bovril if you like. I managed to wangle a towel at the "baths" (a matter of 10 miles march) before I got yours. Thank all and sundry for the various contributions to the parcels. Sorry the kiddies are not overgrand. Tell Kitty not to count on my getting wounded. Had a chap buried by a shell the other day, but only shaken a bit.

'Well ta ta once more. Plenty of love when it can find outward expression. Here's to the time when Old Bill chucks his mit in.'

'*6 December*. Dear Madame, It is with my deepest regret that I write these few lines to inform you that your husband has died of wounds received in action on Saturday morning 4 December. He was shot in the back whilst carrying out his duties in charge of his gun. He was quite cheerful when he was carried to the dressing station. We did not think it was as bad as it has turned out to be and we were all very much shocked to hear that he had passed away. No one is more sorry to lose him as I am. He was one of the best lads that I had in my section and we shall miss him very much. Again I tender to you my deepest sympathy in your very sad bereavement. Believe me to be yours very sincerely, Sgt W. Rudlin.'

Mrs Boorer never got over her grief, and her son and

daughter are convinced that it led to her early death, at the age of fifty-two. She died after an air raid, in a house in Catford near where she was living when the news of her husband's death arrived. 'She once told us that her father had intercepted the letter and tried to soften the shock,' recalls John Boorer, a senior civil servant in the Department of Health and Social Security. 'By all accounts they were a very devoted couple. When we were young, of course, she had little time to brood and dedicated her life to bringing us up. It was a hard struggle on her widow's pension. She took a job for a time as caretaker in a house evacuated by a wealthy family because of the Zeppelin raids. Later we had lodgers. She also took in sewing and I can remember more than once seeing her crying as she sewed late into the night.'

'She remained devoted to father's memory, though she did not often talk about him to us,' says Mrs Goddard. 'When my brothers had reached the boisterous stage she would sometimes say: "They need a father now they're boys." But she turned down an offer of marriage. Her grief was bottled up and when my brothers were called up in the last war she became very tense and bitter about life.'

Ten letters of condolence were found in Mrs Boorer's deed box. They at least would have given a kind of comfort immediately after her husband's death in the knowledge that she had not been left to grieve alone. One was from Mrs Gladys Penn, wife of his company officer, who was helping run a society organised by officers and their wives with the aim of helping soldiers' wives in need.

Shortly after Boorer's arrival in France, Mrs Penn had written: 'We are all facing a very anxious time and it will be so nice if you feel that you can count on me as one who takes an interest in all that concerns you, in the same way that I know my husband does in your husband, both as an individual and as a member of his company.' Now, on black-edged notepaper, she wrote: 'I cannot *tell* you how grieved I am to hear your

news or how sorry I am for you—I only wish I could do something to try and help you, but I know nobody can—I cannot
tell you how *dreadfully sorry* I am for you and how I am thinking
of you . . .'

Lieutenant Cuthbert Ellison, his section officer, wrote: 'I
write to sympathise with you on the loss of your husband, he
was buried just off La Bassée road. I will see that his grave is
properly looked after. I do not think he suffered much. I hear
he was very cheerful. I am afraid I did not see him myself. He
is a great loss to me as he was a splendid soldier and had a
splendid character. Will you please let me know if there is
anything I can do for you . . .'

A week later Lieutenant Ellison's mother wrote: 'I sent your
letter on to my son. He has told me how truly he is feeling for
you and the children. He did not know how old they were but
asked me to send some chocolates. Please let me know if there
is anything I can do for you. Cuthbert was wounded a fortnight ago but very slight and is back in the trenches. I do feel
SO sorry for you and the children . . .'

A wounded guardsman wrote from a London military
hospital (where Mrs Boorer evidently later visited him): 'It is
quite right what Mrs Penfold told you, I was in the same dressing station as your husband before he died. I am afraid that I
cannot tell you very much though, as I was only a few minutes
with him but I shall very willingly tell you all I can when you
call. I was in the same company as your dear husband and
cannot tell you how very sorry I was to see him pass to the great
unknown. He was very popular with all of us and I can truly
say that he was a proper decent and straightforward man in
every way and I can assure you that all our hearts go to you
with feelings of the deepest sorrow and sympathy in your great
loss . . .'

The two letters Mrs Boorer must have returned to most were
from soldiers unused to expressing themselves in the written
word—Lance-Corporal A. Hosted, who was in charge of

C

Boorer's machine-gun at the time he was shot, and her two brothers, Tom and Jim Moore, who were serving on another sector of the front.

Lance-Corporal Hosted wrote: '. . . He was shot about five yards away from me and believe me Mrs I had him inside the trench and had his wound bandaged up and on the stretcher and on his way to the station in a quarter of an hour, he bore up very bravely I hardly thought it was really so bad. When I helped him on the stretcher he smiled at me and said: "Do you think it is Blighty [England] for me Corporal Hosted?" I said, "Yes old lad it is," and he promised to drop me a line. I was quite surprised when I came out of the trenches and heard of his death. I am very sorry for you and the children he was the best man on my gun. I do not know if you know it, it was a sniper's bullet did it while we were filling sandbags and I am pleased to say they are looking after his grave here . . .'

Mrs Boorer's brothers, Tom and Jim, were (according to what John Boorer learned) the 'rough and ready' ones of her large family. Jim was later in the war to see his brother blown to pieces by a shell. Wounded himself, he survived the war to emigrate to Canada as a farmer. Their pencilled scrawl is more than a fumbling attempt to comfort a sister in her grief. In its stark reference to the shattering effects of trench warfare and the cheapness of life on the Western Front it could stand for any Tommy's strangled cry of anguish at the pity of it all.

'We just got the news and needless to say how sorry we are for you and the kiddies for it is not us fellows that get the blunt of this war but the folks we leave at home, for we do not say much but we know how you feel so you have our sympathy and feeling, but there are times out here when we would rather be gone as to put up with condiscons that we sometimes get out here at times when the Germans are bombarding and the boys get knock over one by one and can't hit back. But it beyond me to explain the scene, you see the boys come along crying like children and shaking like old men, still the shells burst in the

34

air and scatter death and distrackion or a fellow may be in a gay mood and forget there is a war and walk out of cover or straighten himself up (specially if he is a big man) after being cramped in a dugout (for they are not built for comfort) and show himself above the parapet—"bing" go a bullet, maybe catch the man.

'Well Nance let hope for the best, a soldier (Catholic) is forgiven of his sins by dieing on a battlefield so that is a comfort and it is better to be a Dead Hero than living coward. And don't think Bert was inviting it because he joined the Machine-Guns because the boys all volunteer to join that and different things rather than be in the infantry here, for when you are not fighting you are working and it just seems that you will get the dirt. But never mind Dear Girlie you are far braver than us for you have to take what is given but us we can out and forget it and if we goe under we are gone. But we boys will try and help you and Dad will help you too but Dear don't let it spoil your Xmas for it don't do no good for Bert would not like it if he was there. So Dear it must be for the best so Dear as it getting Dark so I will close now. So goodbye for now from your loving brothers, Tom and Jim.'

2 'My Dearest Nell . . .'

'I submit these papers to you hoping someone will elucidate a story of a soldier/sailor of war who lived and died for his country. His letters tell a simple story of a man hanging on to a hope of the future which never materialised.'

This note accompanied a package containing forty-two letters, written by a Royal Marine sergeant between August 1914 and October 1916, when he was killed on the Western Front, which a local resident had found on a council rubbish dump in Lambeth in January 1974 and passed on to the Imperial War Museum. How they came to be on the dump remains a mystery. There is no record of the widow who had preserved them having lived or died in this London borough. But there is no doubt that the museum's Department of Documents is a more suitable depository for them than a council incinerator. They are a rare find.

The letters were written by Marine Sergeant Bert James Fielder to his wife Nell during his three years away from their home in Deal, a home he was not to see again. They are love letters as much as war letters. Loving concern for his dearest Nell and their young son, intensified by the threat of air raids and shelling that Deal was subjected to, underlines all he writes. It is a love none the less moving for being stumblingly expressed. And the occasional homilies he addresses to his wife read like a deliberate stiffening of the sinews: 'We are not only

fighting for our present happiness, but fighting for the generation that is to come into the world, which take our place when
we are gone, these little ones will never forget us when they
grow up, when they read in history of these terrible times when
their fathers were fighting and mothers were living in a terrible
agony in the old home . . .'

Fielder served for a brief spell, until he was wounded, in the
trenches at Gallipoli, and his letter hinting at the savagery of
the fighting there was written some time later, when he could
assure his wife that he was unlikely to return to a fighting front.
But the letters, though mostly written from backwaters of the
war, have an interest beyond the context of time and place. The
simple story they tell of a soldier dreaming of home is as old as
history. Fielder was a regular and there is no element of self-
pity in the homesickness he expresses. He is sustained by an
ingrained sense of duty and patriotism. The war for him,
however tragic, was a just and inevitable one.

The letters had only just been received at the Imperial War
Museum when they were handed to me for perusal by Roderick
Suddaby, head of the Department of Documents: 'Found on a
rubbish dump—but you never know . . .' They were in a brown
paper bag, jumbled up in no chronological order, written in
pencil in a firm if somewhat laboured hand. I dipped in at
random.

'. . . You say that when my last letter came you was sitting
by the fire brooding and thinking of me that Sunday morning
when we left Deal, my dear Scrumps, I wonder how often I
think of it too, when I had to motion you and the Boy back, I
can tell you I had a pretty big lump in my throat . . .'

'. . . So his latest craze is fishing is it, yes I'm afraid I'm
missing a lot of his amusing little ways but I shall make up for
it when I get home, oh that glorious day when the boys *do* get
home . . .'

'. . . Please don't cry so much when you write next, as it
makes them in an awful mess . . .'

37

The handwriting had become familiar, there was a feeling of eavesdropping on a private, intimate conversation between two living people, when I came across an envelope addressed in another hand. The letter was neatly written on one side of a piece of notepaper, dated 30 October 1916, from France: 'Dear Madam, I am very sorry to have to tell you that Sergeant Fielder, B. J., 15388 RMLI, died in No 11 Casualty Clearing Station last night. He was admitted during the day severely wounded in thigh and foot and from the first there was almost no hope of his recovery . . .'

With no premonition that this was to be the abrupt end to all that loving concern, all those buoyant promises of a safe homecoming and a life of contentment after the war, that letter seemed to cry aloud again its brutal extinction of hope.

Bereavement was commonplace in a war in which nearly a million men in the British forces lost their lives and is taken for granted by the chronicler of those tragic times. The spotlight is on the men in the trenches rather than the women who waited, in daily hope and dread of the postman's knock. But in the letters of Sergeant Fielder, as of Guardsman Boorer, one can see how closely linked were the two and how the Tommy was as much concerned about what his wife was going through as she about him. That gallant tribute from Kathleen Boorer's brothers—'you are far braver than us for you have to take what is given'—is echoed in Fielder's recognition of the lonely wives and mothers 'living in a terrible agony in the old home'. One wonders what cold comfort Nell Fielder might have drawn from the exhortation contained in that letter as she read it again in her widowhood.

The few documents to be found among the letters, together with the brief record of Fielder's service in the Royal Marine archives, provide only the sketchiest of backgrounds. Even here there is a discrepancy. Born in Sheerness, Kent, son of a sailor, Fielder is officially recorded as having enlisted in the Marines in 1897 at the age of seventeen (his occupation at that time given as 'barman'), while his marriage certificate, in 1909, gives his age as twenty-seven. It could be that he was keen enough to enlist to have pretended to have been older than he was.

His bride at St Luke's Church, Ramsgate, was Helenor Elizabeth Woodward, aged twenty-five, daughter of a brick-maker. He was based at Walmer Barracks, Deal, and their home was at 5 Granville Terrace, a street that no longer exists. The only documents dating from after his death are a 'notification of discharge', in August 1919, revealing that Nell Fielder had joined the WRNS, and a claim for retirement pension indicating that she was still alive and living in Deal in 1954. No relatives have been traceable, and there is no clue as to whether Bert Fielder, so frequently and lovingly referred to in his father's letters as 'the Boy', is still alive.

During World War I the Royal Marines, whose training in peacetime had been basically as an adjunct to the Navy, manning the guns of the Fleet and acting as landing parties, played an increasing role in the land fighting. Fielder's early reference to being fitted with khaki uniform marks the formation of the Royal Marine Brigade, in which he was later to find himself in the thick of the fighting at Gallipoli.

Fielder's letters to his 'dear (or dearest) Nell' almost invariably end with the same rather stiff flourish: 'I think this is about all I've got to say at present so will conclude with love to you both I remain your ever loving husband, Bert.' The early ones are written from a Marines' barracks at Gosport, Hants, and they indicate the elation and high sense of purpose with which Britain went to war, in the confident belief that it would soon be over. The first is dated 4 August 1914, the day war was declared, though evidently written before that momentous news had reached the barracks.

'We arrived here at 12.30 midnight on Monday after a very bad journey with nothing but stoppages. All the stations along the line were crowded with Soldiers, Sailors and Marines on the active list and pensioners and reserves joining their divisions, also crowds of civilians leaving the different seaside resorts to get back to their homes, and foreigners going back to their country, one train was full up with Italians going back. So you can guess what sort of a state the railways was in, and yet it seemed marvellous how cool and calm everyone appeared to be. Sometimes it was quite funny to see some of the old pensioners hurry back dressed in all sorts of clothes, half uniform and half civilian clothes on, one Marine at the Union Jack Club was setting down to his tea with all uniform on and *a bowler hat on his head,* he had travelled up from the other side of London like it. At Waterloo Station there was nothing else but cheering the whole time we were waiting for the train. When we got to a place called Winchester a few miles from Gosport we heard that the Government had taken over the railways at 12 o'clock that night. The latest news we have here is the same as you see in the papers, that is that England won't go to war unless Germany sends down her fleet to bombard the French coast or tries to get at France by going through Belgium . . .'

'*6 August* . . . So the Boy woke up in the night crying for me, I expect he will soon get used to not seeing me at home. My dear Nell, I don't think this war is going to be half as bad as people expected it to be, you see it is not a hard job for England, so there is no need to worry yourself, as long as I can keep you informed as to where I am it will be alright . . .'

'*12 August* . . . There is a possibility of us going to a very desolate place by name of Skappa Flow. The Admiralty is taking this place over in the event of a big naval war as a big stores place, the reason is that these towns down this end of England are too handy for German warships which may nip out of their harbours at any time and blow up or capture some of the stores which are required for our own Men-of-War, so the idea is that they are sending this Battalion of 500 Marines with 6 field guns to protect it.

'Plenty of rifle firing and marching this last two days, the Btn seems to be pretty fit with the exception of one or two which can't shoot or have fallen out on the march and these have been taken out and other men put in their place, but they stick it pretty well considering a good many are men on the shady side of fifty. I am very glad to say that my shooting has not suffered at all through not having any practice, I was quite impressed how well I did. Every day we come in from a march we have to wash our feet and the doctor comes round the barrack rooms and inspects them, any man with a sign of tenderness or a red patch on his foot showing any signs of chafing is sent to the hospital straight away to have them seen to, so that will just tell you what a state of perfection they mean to get us.

'Should very much like to see my little wife and the Boy, but what's the good of building up hope for the present until I know what's to be done, the only thing to do is live in hopes and look at the bright side of things with a cheerful face . . . PS Please give my kindest regards to Mr and Mrs Evclegh and tell them that the Germans are not likely to worry Deal just yet.'

'*15 August* . . . No further news of going away but we are still making every preparation to get ready for hard work. Today the Btn has been measured for a suit of khaki each, and they have also started issuing the identification discs, these are little copper plates, one given to each man, which is sewn on the inside of his jacket, and this plate has on it the name of the man, his next of kin and other particulars . . . I am scribbling a few lines to the Boy on his piece of paper . . .'

The letter from Fielder's son reads: 'My dear Daddy, I hope you are well and soon going to send me my big gun. Auntie Emily is hear and going to take me to throw stones in the water to morrow. dear daddy I went and fed my bunnie rabbit, it is growing a big chap. Now I am just going to bed. Good night. Love from Bertie. XXXX (all for Daddy).'

'Dear Sonny, Mummy tells me in the letter that your cold is

getting better, I am very glad to hear it, also that your rabbits are getting on so fine. How did you like your pictures of the Man-of-War and the Waterplane, I will send you some more when I see some in the shops. I am sending you a penny in this letter for yourself to spend at the toyshop. For Sonny XXXX.'

'*17 August* . . . If I go away you must not worry if you don't get my letters, because you must understand it is all for the Good of England, and the English Soldier is not only fighting for his country but to save his own *home* from destruction and being ruled over by the Germans. My dear Nell, you ask me if our people have started fighting yet, yes it was officially announced in the papers last week that the British force were working with the Belgians at the town of Liege. A telegram stuck up in the PO last night said there had been more fighting but no British killed or wounded, these Germans are getting an awful licking according to accounts. I cannot tell you how long it will last but Lord Kitchener says it will be a long war and is making preparations for one . . .'

Fielder's next two letters refer briefly to the Royal Marine Brigade's participation in the early stages of the war in Belgium and France. With news that German patrols were nearing Ostend, it landed there on 28 August, but no action ensued and the Brigade was recalled a week later. On 19 September the Brigade landed at Dunkirk in a bid to save the Channel ports. The Commander Samson to whom Fielder refers was in charge of a force of armoured cars harassing the German right flank and operating against the German air bases nearest to England.

The brevity of Fielder's letter after the Ostend excursion was no doubt because a home leave was in the offing.

'*4 September*. Did you get the card sent on way to Belgium, and two I sent when landed? I don't think that is me in the picture Annie speaks about, I only caught the camera once when we were landing and that was when I was standing up in the little steamboat and the camera was a cinematograph, so perhaps I shall be on the pictures somewhere or other. So you say you couldn't sleep last night, I expect you'll be able to sleep alright next Saturday night with your old Bert's arms around you "Eh what" . . .'

'*1 October* . . . I am sending this from a little place called Cassell about 25 miles from Dunkirk and 75 miles from the scene of the actual fighting so that you can see that I am safe as houses. The only thing I don't like to think is that you are all needlessly worrying yourself about me, I only wish you would believe me that they will not send us to the Front we are being kept to look after Commander Sampson's aeroplanes, there is nothing in the least to worry about. I am in the very best of health, this life evidently suits me to a T. I am writing this sitting out on a verandah of a small school where we are billeted, it is a lovely sunny afternoon and this place is on top of a high hill and some lovely country is to be seen whichever way you look . . . PS Please don't cry so much when you write next, as it makes them in an awful mess.'

Covering the next ten months only six brief letters have survived, three of them undated and with no indication as to his whereabouts. A letter dated 15 December 1914, indicates that he has just spent another leave at home, possibly his last. All that he refers to about that leave is a misunderstanding with a shopkeeper: 'I am certain that you paid that food bill. I remember you telling me what you had left out of a half-sovereign. Don't you think Mr Norman has made a mistake?'

In an undated letter he writes: 'I am sending you a list of names of different places where we may be sent, each name is numbered so that when I write to you I can look at the number on the list in my pocket book and put it down on the top left-hand corner of the card or letter.' There are forty-one names on his list, mostly in France and Belgium, but also including Gibraltar, Malta, Spain, German East and South-West Africa, Malta, Cyprus, Aden, Alexandria, Cairo. In the event he does not appear to have used this crafty scheme of dodging the censor.

Another undated letter reads: 'Just got your letter dated 23 March in which the first thing you mention is the air raid, so that of course has put my mind at rest, at least until I hear of another raid, but you must not get alarmed at the explosions, as I expect most of them you hear are the anti-aircraft guns and I'm sure I am with you in praying to the One Above that you are both kept safe and sound and that this war will come to a speedy close . . . After this letter it may be some time before you get another, as I believe the *Ionian* is going to Salonika first to drop some troops and then take us on to Mudros.'

Mudros, the great natural harbour on the island of Lemnos, was headquarters of the Mediterranean Expeditionary Force then assembling for the assault on the Gallipoli peninsula. The Royal Marine Brigade was by now part of the Royal Naval Division, which was to play an heroic role in that doomed campaign. And one cannot but regret that Fielder, evidently out of concern for his wife's fears for his safety, wrote so little about his own experiences of the fighting.

On 26 April, the day after the first landings by British, Australian and French troops, he wrote: 'Dear Nell, Just this PC to let you know that everything is alright up to date. I don't expect I shall have an opportunity to let you have another for some time after this, so don't get in a stew if you don't hear, hope you and the Boy are in the best of health, much love Bert.'

There followed five Field Service postcards, dated 3, 5, 10, 13, 19 May intimating only that he was alive. The next news of her husband Nell Fielder received (unless there are letters missing) was on 14 July, a notification from the RND Record Office in London that he had received a gunshot wound in his right shoulder and had been admitted to the military hospital in Cairo on 31 May.

Presuming, from his training at Gosport Barracks, that he was attached to the Portsmouth Battalion of the Royal Marine Brigade, Fielder would have been engaged in some of the bloodiest fighting of the campaign before being wounded.

On 28 April the Portsmouth and Chatham Battalions landed at Anzac, the beach stormed three days before by the Australians, and took over the line in the centre. On 1 May the Turks made a desperate attempt to drive them back into the sea and for twenty-four hours were beaten back by the Marines, firing point-blank into the screaming hordes. A charge up a hill to beat back another attack was described by an Australian officer, a VC, as 'the bravest thing I've seen so far'.

On 12 May the two Marine battalions were switched to the British trenches facing the Turks on Achi Baba, a bald ridge dominating the southern end of the peninsula. It is of the savage but unavailing fighting to capture this vital stronghold that Fielder writes in the only letter that reveals the horrors he had witnessed and the ordeal he had survived. It is dated 21 July and reads as though the memories were already half-buried, only dragged out of him by a slighting comment by his wife on the progress of the campaign. That he had not intended telling her that he had been wounded, let alone of his battle experiences, is clear from his next letter.

'*18 July*. RND Base, Alexandria, Egypt . . . So you say you was worried when you got to know of my being wounded, my dear Scrumps, you need not tell me that because that was the first thing that entered my mind and it was worrying me in case they reported me as seriously wounded or dead, I know that people are reported so by mistake, I asked everybody that I could find who I fancied had anything to do with reporting it home so that I could stop it. But still you need not worry any more about me because I think I am settled here for some time. I get plenty of work, I have to fit up all the wounded that have come out of hospital, because you know they lose everything when they leave Gallipoli to come to hospital (except their identification discs which they wear round their necks) so of course they have got to be got ready for the field again.

'I have only 2 Storemen to help me, and I am jack of all trades, Armourer Sgt., QMS and Clerk all in one. I commence

45

work at 6 and finish at 8 or sometimes 9 . . . How is the Boy
getting on, you tell me that when my Field postcards came he
wanted to know what daddy said of his ship. Poor little Kid!
I expect he was disappointed. Why didn't you fake up some
imaginary writing on the postcard, but anyhow I think I remember sending him a ship when in hospital . . .'

'*21 July* . . . I think I may be able to keep here a few weeks
yet, anyhow I've got hopes of staying until the Dardanelles job
is over . . . You ask me when the war is going to be over. Well, I
will just tell you, only keep it secret. *In October.* You say we
don't seem to be getting on very well out here; My Word if you
only knew what a job we've got before us, just try to imagine a
hill called Achi Baba, just fancy yourself at the bottom of a big
hill with trenches and trenches piled on top of one another,
made of concrete with thousands of Turks and machine-guns,
five of these trenches we took one morning one after the other,
but before we got to the first trench we left a good many of our
chums behind, but it's no good stopping and the faster you can
run the better chance you have of getting through the rain of
bullets, and our boys went mad.

'I have thought just lately what a lot of savages war turns us
into, we see the most horrible sights of bloodshed and simply
laugh at it. It seems to be nothing but blood, blood everywhere
you go and on everything you touch, and you are walking
amongst dead bodies all day and all night, human life seems to
be of no value at all—you are joking with a chap one minute
and the next minute you go to the back of the trench to do a
job for yourself and then you see a little mound of earth with a
little rough wooden cross on it with the name of the man you
had been joking with a short time before. My dear Scrumps,
I don't know whether I'm right in telling you this, because you
worry so but I would not mention it only for the reason that I
don't think I shall have any more of it, but I certainly *do* thank
the One Above and you for your prayers at night together with
our Boy for keeping me safe throughout it all.

46

'Always you are both in my thoughts, I think of you both in that little kitchen by yourselves and know that you are thinking of me and wondering perhaps if you will ever see me come back again, every night at nine o'clock out here which is seven o'clock in England, I think that it is the Boy's bedtime and I always can picture him kneeling in his cot saying his prayers after Mummy. But "Cheer up", my Scrumps, this will all end soon and we shall be together again and carry on the old life once more.

'My dear Scrumps, I wonder if the Boy still thinks of the gun I promised to bring him home, I got hold of two Turks' guns to bring home and after keeping them for about two weeks, I got wounded and then of course I lost them as I did everything else. I might also say that the Deal Battalion have all lost their bags again, they were coming from the ship in a barge and a Turk shell hit the barge, so they sank to the bottom of the Dardanelles. The Naval Division is pretty well cut up, especially the Marines, they can only make 3 btns out of 4 even after the last lot came out from England. I think there is some move on to withdraw the Marines and Naval Division from the Dardanelles also the other troops which were in the first part of the fighting as they are in a bad state and I expect we'll get a quiet job as garrison for some place. I expect by this time you have got General Hamilton's report of the fighting here, my dear Scrumps I think I will wind up now as I've just looked at the watch and its a quarter to eleven. I've been writing ever since nine o'clock, so Night Night and God Bless you . . .'

'*29 July*. I have received your parcel dated 25 May, when I cut the cake it had gone mouldy right through the middle, but anyhow the tobacco was VERY acceptable, also the chocs etc. I am glad to know that the Boy looks smart, I am anxiously waiting for his photo, I was going to suggest that you be taken yourself, but WE don't alter so much in six months as kiddies would . . .

'So you say you have got plenty of soldiers there and so

47

there are out here and everywhere else, I think this newspaper talk is all Bunkum about not having enough soldiers now, it looks to me as if we are simply playing a waiting game so as to wear Germany out and make them cry for peace. According to what I can make out from the papers all the German army is trying to get Warsaw (WHICH THEY WON'T) after that they will turn their attention on France and try the hardest they have ever tried to get through to Calais and that will be the finish of them, and a d—— good job too because I'm tired of being away from "My little grey home in the West".

'I expect the Bull and George looks a pretty sight, you say that if anyone had been in the cellar they would have been killed but you see all the bombs don't go right through, they sometimes only go through the roof. I am glad you enjoyed yourself at Dover and hope you will go in for a little bit of pleasure because if you can only manage to forget your troubles for half an hour it will do you the world of good, especially if you can manage a good laugh. It is quite true what you see in the papers about the Turks being short of ammunition, we have known it here a long time. My dear Scrumps, I have sent you a parcel with some thick underclothing in, which I thought would come in handy for winter, or if you like you can make Father a present of them, if you think they would be of no use to me. I am trying to send on another later, it is all spare stuff which only lumbers up the store and I can't get rid of it . . .'

'*26 September* . . . The weather here has just begun to turn and it has been quite cold today, my shoulder has been giving me "Gee up", I don't know what it will be like during the winter at home, it seems a funny feeling in it and my arm goes quite numb from the shoulder to the finger tips, but I expect it will wear off in time . . . As regards the news of the Zeps, I have heard the same news from everybody who have had letters from home, of course it is very terrible but it will teach people at home to appreciate the men that have got to live in it from one month's end to the other. I think you've got the laugh of old

48

Page 49 (*above left*) Guardsman Boorer; (*above right*) Midshipman Drewry, taken from a group on Gallipoli beach; (*below left*) Captain Nightingale; (*below right*) Captain Martin, taken some time after the Siege of Kut

Page 50   (above) The Guards Brigade in France before the Battle of Loos;
(below) Trooper Case, Royal Wiltshire Yeomanry, in full marching order,
showing the weight of equipment carried by mounted troops

Em, I can just imagine her being scared, tell her she must put her umbrella up to keep them off . . . I've just seen a paper that a Hun aeroplane dropped on Gallipoli, telling the British to surrender, and a lot more nonsense, which everyone knows to be lies, I will try to get you a copy and send it on . . .'

'*8 November.* Another week has rolled on and as each one goes I keep thinking how cold it must be getting in England and how it compares to the weather we are getting here. I expect everyone at home is wearing thick winter clothing while we are still wearing our light drill khaki. I stretched a point last night and went to see the pictures, they showed all the guns that were captured in the last big advance, and a review of the French troops by General Joffre, and last but not least a film of Charlie Chaplin. It was the first time I had been out of the camp for 3 months.

'I think you mistake my meaning when I said in my last that I wouldn't mind if the war went on for another year, of course I should like it to finish tomorrow but I should like it to finish properly, that is that Germany gets such a smashing that she won't be able to try the experiment again for a good many years, not during our lifetime or our Boy's lifetime, you see it's no use to indulge in selfish thoughts, that is thinking of your own happiness, we are not only fighting for our present happiness, but fighting for the generation that is to come into the world, which take our place when we are gone, these little ones will never forget us when they grow up, when they read in history of these terrible times when their fathers were fighting and mothers were living in a terrible agony in the old home, oh yes, let it go on, until this race of Evil Human Devils are wiped off the face of God's earth.

'Yes, My dear Nell, this must go on, if we stopped now we should fall short of doing our duty to the thousands of poor fellows who have gone, and their lives would have been given in vain. No doubt you will think I am getting sentimental but these thoughts are from the bottom of my heart, and I should not mention it only for the fact that I know YOU will listen to them in a sympathetic light, more so than anyone else I could tell in this world. So when I say, let it go on, you will understand what I mean. We have nothing to complain of, I am quite safe here and you and the Boy are getting your food, the fact of about five thousand miles separating us is the only trouble and what is that to what some people have lost in this great struggle . . .'

'*10 October* . . . I've had a cold ever since I left the trenches, the whole of the time I was at the Front I never had the slightest cold I never knew what it was like to have a cold in the trenches and I never felt in better health but as soon as I got to hospital the doctor put me in bed as though I'd got malaria fever but it was only a bad cold, so that just shows what effect being constantly in the fresh air had on me, although I did expect to get a cold or two considering the times we got wet through and slept in it and dried on and got wet again . . .'

'*15 November* . . . Tell the Boy I thank him for his ship which he drew on thick paper, so you say he is getting a bit out of hand, you must put your foot down and when you tell him to do anything *make him do it*, or else punish him, of course I don't mean beat him, but such as keeping him in all day or putting him to bed before time, such as that. Of course it is only natural that he will be getting out of hand to a certain extent, but you must deal with him firmly it is for his sake that you bring him up properly now, or else when he grows older he will have no respect for breaking the laws of the country no more than he does the laws that you impose on him in his young days . . . I expect you find it rather nippy when you turn out to feed the chickens in the morning, I suppose you will soon be killing them for Xmas . . .'

'*22 November* . . . You must tell the Boy from me that he has got to be a good Boy and do as Mummy tells him or else Daddy won't buy him that gun he promised him when he comes home . . . So you don't know what is the matter with the people down the street. Who are they? Why should they treat you like dirt? Are they some of those that haven't got anyone at the Front? If so I expect you have been giving them a bit of your mind with reference to the fact that your "Old Man" is doing their country's work for some of them, but you mustn't forget that I'm not the only one by a long way . . .'

'*29 November.* Our rainy season has just commenced, it's been raining heavens hard all day, I keep thinking of the poor devils in the trenches as I remember my own experiences and it was much warmer than it is now up there . . . So you are going to tea with Mrs Wilson, now don't forget the advice I've given you before, go very carefully and find out your new friends before you get too intimate with them. But still as you say I don't want you to keep away from everybody or else you and the Boy will get melancholy. I'm glad to know that the Boy is getting fatter, I certainly think he can do with a little more fat, feed him on fatty foods but not so much as to turn him up. So his latest craze is fishing is it, yes I'm afraid I'm missing a lot of his amusing little ways, but I shall make up for it when I get home, oh that glorious time when the boys *do* get home. But I shall always be pleased to read of any accounts you can send me of him, as I fancy I'm at home when I read about him . . .'

'*7 December* . . . So you say the Boy likes Charlie Chaplin. Yes, I expect he does, but you must be careful he doesn't catch cold coming out of those close places. I wonder if he still thinks of the romps he used to have with Daddy each night before he went to bed. My goodness, it seems ages ago to me! You say that when my last letter came you was sitting by the fire brooding and thinking of me that Sunday morning when we left Deal, my dear Scrumps, I wonder how often I think of it too, when I had to motion you and the Boy back, I can tell you I had a pretty big lump in my throat. I don't know what my feelings would have been or yours either if we had only known what we had to go through in the near future. But still, my dear Nell, you hadn't better let me catch you brooding because you don't know I may sneak around the back way to surprise you one of these fine days . . .

'Here am I on to my third sheet of paper and I haven't said anything about the war yet. But there is one thing I must tell you we consider it a joke. Well, two months ago we had a chap from the trenches very bad with *Sunstroke*, he got better and went to the trenches again, last week we saw the same chap down here again, but with *Frostbite* this time! So you see he'd had two extremes, they say it's very nippy on the "Pennins" now . . .'

'*4 February 1916* . . . How is the old stocking looking up, I should say it is full to bursting point by now as you have not had a hungry Old Man to keep this last 13 months. My Word he'll have to make up for lost time when he *does* get home so look out and get a full pantry by about Easter, and won't it be strange to sleep in a spring bed with a long haired chum beside him, "What ho" what do you say to breakfast in bed first day, "Eh what" that will make you laugh. I wonder what the Boy will say I expect he will be very shy of me for a little. I expect you are anxious to know how MY stocking is looking up, well as I've no Old Woman to do my sewing it has got a big hole in the toe, as a consequence all the "Moosh" falls out as soon as I put it in, but I think I can rake enough up to take you for a month's holiday and enjoy ourselves after the war. PS I hope you have not had the Zeps.'

'*7 February* . . . I'm glad to see they published in the papers the towns where the Zeps visited because I was rather worried when I first saw that they had paid another visit to England and I was greatly relieved when I saw the paper next day . . .'

'*9 February* . . . I suppose you was terribly scared over the aeroplane raid and no doubt you wish for all this to be over, but how about the men at the front who have bombs bursting and bullets flying around all day long without a moment's peace, can you wonder at them being sent home with their nerves wrecked . . .'

54

'*15 February* . . . Just seen this morning's papers which tell us about the air raid on Walmer and one Marine being wounded, thank goodness it is no worse. I hope you was not anywhere near it, you must keep your ears open for them coming and take cover . . .'

'*7 March*. Now what do you think of the latest news. It seems to be the general opinion here that the end is not far off. Someone has just said it appeared in the papers that Lord Kitchener has said that the war will last 80 days from the beginning of the Battle of Verdun . . .'

'*18 March* . . . What sort of weather are you getting at Deal now, pretty parky I expect and plenty of March winds, it makes me shiver to think of it. "What ho" the little fireplace with the top up and feet in the oven for a footwarmer before we go to bed, I am longing for the good old time to come again, once I get home it will take more than Wild Horses to drag me away again. But never mind I suppose the time will come if only we have enough patience. Today we have had a bit of change in the weather, it's blowing great guns and you can hear the waves roaring over the rocks on the seashore, it started this morning with a sandstorm and has been raining on and off all day which helps to keep the sand down . . .'

'*22 March*. It's very annoying to have our mails sent all over the place especially as a letter is the only means we have of getting the exact locality of these air raids, you can just imagine what a stew I get in when it is in the papers with only just the town mentioned, it means that I've got to wait in suspense at least 2 weeks before I can be at all sure that you are safe. Just think there was only one of our machines went up, I think our Flying Corps at home wants shaking up a bit, I suppose the poor chaps were having their Sunday afternoon nap or else they were at dinner and could not be interrupted, but anyhow I reckon the German planes were there long enough for at least about 20 of our machines to go up after them.

'We have it here in the paper about the *Maloza* going down

55

off Deal, fancy posting a letter at Deal which goes to London and then comes back to Deal in that manner. My dear Scrumps, you say that as regards to the air raid that "*the married square just at the corner caught it*", now I wonder if you mean to say that part of the building was knocked down or that only the windows were blown in, and whereabouts did the bomb drop? . . .

'One thing I've been going to ask you, isn't the Boy supposed to go to school at five years or is it six, I don't want him to go until I get home. Try and keep him until then. I'm very glad to know he is in good health, is he getting any fatter? I think it is nearly time he had his photo taken again because if you remember we said long ago that we would have it taken every six months and I'm rather anxious to see any alterations in him while I'm away. You did not tell me in your letter if he got his birthday card and what he said of it, perhaps it is in the letter that is lying under the sea off Deal. Ask the Boy if he would like to have a box with Daddy like he used to. I've got a Turk gun for him if I can only get it home, but don't tell him in case I can't get home and he would be disappointed . . .'

On 13 April Fielder wrote from Mudros where the Royal Naval Division were assembled awaiting their next move. Since the evacuation of Gallipoli at the end of 1915 it had remained in the Eastern Mediterranean while its future was discussed in London. It was now decided to send it to the Western Front in preparation for the British offensive on the Somme which it was confidently hoped would turn the tide of the war. When they set sail from Mudros Fielder was buoyed up by the hope of ten days' leave when all those dreams of home would come true.

When they arrived in France the Division was reorganised and renamed the 63rd (Royal Naval) Division. Fielder, who in Alexandria had been promoted to Acting Quartermaster Sergeant, became a sergeant again, attached to the Hood Battalion, commanded (as he mentions) by Colonel Arthur

Asquith, son of the Prime Minister. On the eve of Gallipoli
Asquith had been one of the seven young officers picked to
attend the burial, on the island of Skyros, of the Royal Naval
Division's most celebrated officer, Rupert Brooke. As in Brooke's
poem, 'The Soldier', Fielder was to get no closer to home than
'some corner of a foreign field'.

'*26 June*. I am now in billets in a farmhouse in a village called
Dieval near Lens about 25 miles from the firing-line, but rest
assured that I am quite safe as the battalion is a new one and is
to have about three months training as soon as we get more to
join it, which will be some time yet. You will notice I have
gone back to sgt but I am expecting to get made company sgt
in two or three days. That is what the Colonel has promised me
if I suit him. I am the only Marine in the btn and the Colonel is
Mr Asquith the eldest son of Mr Asquith the Prime Minister, so
if I can settle in this btn I shall be in luck once more . . .

'I am pretty busy at present as I have taken over company
sgt-major, of a brand new coy, and you can bet there is some
hard work to do until I can get it into some shape. I wonder
what news you are getting in England. I think something is
doing here as I lay awake last night listening to those big guns
of ours going off around Lens, I think the Germans are at last
getting a strafing.'

'*27 July*. I've been doing night work, I have to go to a place
some miles from here each evening and don't get back until
sometimes 4 in the morning, of course I don't walk it but the
riding in the night air does not improve my cold. One good
thing is we have had the last six days without rain, it is quite a
change to be choked with dust from the road instead of the
usual coating of mud, but I suppose all the troubles will come
to an end "Après la guerre" as the French people say. Don't
keep the Boy from school more than you can possibly help, if he
once gets in the habit of staying away you will have a rare job
to get him to go again . . .'

'*26 September*. Yes this is my third birthday away from home and I am having a day off on the strength of it, or rather it has happened by chance. Yesterday while returning from Field Exercise I jumped down a bank a bit awkward and sprained my right ankle, the result is I'm struck off all duties for the day by order of the doc, but quite expect to be fit tomorrow. What a strange thing that it is exactly eight years ago this month I was in the hospital with the same injury only caused through playing football.

'We got the news here yesterday about the Zep raid, surely it is about time "Kaiser Bill" found out that that game is not worth the candle . . . Yes, the leave has commenced, but only very small numbers are going at a time, you see the people that have been on the peninsula the whole time are going first, and it won't be my turn for a long time yet.'

'*12 October*. What sort of weather are you getting, it is very windy here today, some more rain about I expect which means sticking to the tent all day, but we've got a gramophone to while away the time and plenty of books to read, so you see we don't do so bad. How is the Boy getting on with his schooling, ask him from me when he is going to write Daddy that letter. I think this is all I've got to say at present, shall be very glad when I can write you a long letter, but still we must be patient and wait a little longer.'

Fielder's last letter was written four days before his death. The Somme offensive, launched on 1 July, had degenerated into a pointless war of attrition, in which his battalion was by now engaged. It was not until 13 November that the new 63rd Division were to go into action for the first time in the Battle of the Ancre, the last battle of the offensive, and all was relatively quiet on the Western Front. For Nell Fielder it must have been a lasting agony to know, from her husband's last letter, that he could have been home on compassionate leave at the time he was killed.

'*26 October*. Your letter of the 15th received yesterday noon and those of 16th and 18th last night. It is a pity that you did not let me know of Mother's illness by sending a wire as I have been informed by the OC Coy that I could have had a special leave.

'Am sorry I have not been able to write this last week but we've been in a terrible muddle, not been able to settle anywhere, have had a short stay in the trenches and am now back again for a short rest, and a very much needed clean up, for I can tell you there is *some* mud here at present. Am glad you are both keeping well, am in the pink myself except for a cold which of course is not to be wondered at whilst this wet weather lasts. Hoping this will find you still in the best of health, I must conclude with lots of love from your loving Husband, Bert. XXXXXX.'

'*30 October*. Dear Madam, I am very sorry to have to tell you that Sergeant Fielder, B. J., 15388 RMLI, died in No 11 Casualty Clearing Station last night. He was admitted during the day severely wounded in thigh and foot and from the first there was almost no hope of his recovery. He was unconscious till the evening when he gave us your address, but that was practically all we could get out of him. It was found necessary to operate in the afternoon and his right leg had to be taken off. He had every care and attention possible but in spite of everything he gradually sank and passed quietly away during the night. His wounds were so numerous and at the same time so serious that it was almost hopeless from the first. With *deepest* sympathy in your bereavement, Yours faithfully, Sister-in-Charge.'

Three days later came a letter from the Casualty Clearing Station Chaplain. At the top he has written '*All Saints' Day*'.

'Just a line to express my deepest sympathy with you in your great loss. Your husband was only in this hospital a short time and was unconscious so that I was unable to have any conversation with him. All Saints' Day brings a ray of comfort to the bereaved, leading our thoughts to the time when we hope one day to meet those loved ones who have gone before. I am sure

59

he was a fine fellow and it must be some comfort to feel that he gave up his life for his country. I buried him with the same old service that we use at home in a little cemetery for English soldiers. Excuse more as I am very busy, Very sincerely yours, H. L. Connor, Chaplain.

'PTO. A little cross marks the grave where he was buried and it is registered so that you will be able to find it after the war.'

In the brief official record of Fielder's service with the Royal Marines, his grave is precisely located: '$\frac{1}{4}$ mile NNW of Albert, $3\frac{1}{4}$ miles N of Warloy Baillon, Map reference (A) 2–9.' Tucked among his letters was a small brochure, sent to war widows after the Armistice, giving information about the military cemeteries in France. But there is no knowing if Nell ever went to see the last resting place of her ever loving husband.

3 *Midshipman Drewry VC*

'Young Midshipman Wins the VC: The Immortal story of the
Landing from the River Clyde,' reads the banner headline
across the front page of the *Daily Mirror* for 17 August 1915.
Underneath it a half-page 'exclusive' picture shows Midshipman George Leslie Drewry, RNR, seated on a rocky beach, his
head swathed in bandages. He sits with hands clasping his
knees, seemingly oblivious of the camera, a strained and
haunted look in his far-focused eyes.

'The story of HMS *River Clyde* will be immortal and her name
for ever associated with deeds of the most glorious heroism,'
confidently asserts the caption under the picture. 'When the
vessel, a troopship, was deliberately run aground at the Dardanelles, the lighters which were to form a bridge broke adrift,
so Commander Edward Unwin, RN, and Midshipman Drewry
(both awarded the VC) left the vessel under a murderous fire
to get the lighters into position. Drewry, who is little more than
a boy, was wounded in the head, but continued his work, and
twice subsequently attempted to swim from lighter to lighter
with a line.'

Another midshipman and two seamen were also awarded the
VC, an unprecedented total for a single action. But it was
Drewry whom the papers seized upon as the hero of the hour—
young, handsome, dauntless. At a time when the war on the

Western Front was bogged down it was good to be reminded that deeds of youthful valour were still being performed, that the Nelson touch still flourished.

A frayed and brittle copy of that *Daily Mirror* has been preserved over the years by Ralph Drewry, youngest and last surviving of four Drewry brothers, together with four long letters written by George to his father from Gallipoli. The first gives a detailed account of the part he played in the *River Clyde* landing, and it is illuminating to compare it with the way it was presented in the 'largest circulation picture paper in the world'. The gulf that existed between the man at the front and the civilian back home, who had little conception of what the fighting was really like, is often referred to in the diaries and journals of participants. And it may well have been that the knowledge that what they were experiencing was largely incommunicable to anyone who had not shared it had an inhibiting effect on the writing of letters. Drewry's letters are the kind that any parent following the course of the war in the jingoistic pages of a popular newspaper would have been proud to receive. They give little indication of his innermost feelings at the time. Only in the haunted eyes of that photograph can one guess at the horrors.

Daily Mirror readers that August day were in another world from the fighting front. Vice-Admiral de Robeck's dispatch on the Gallipoli landings of 25 April provided stirring reading, with a strong and varied cast of army and navy heroes, headed by the 'little-more-than-a-boy' Midshipman Drewry (he was actually twenty). The rest of the war news is disposed of in one out of the paper's twelve pages, dominated by a 'spiteful but futile raid' on Whitehaven in Cumberland, when a German submarine fired a few innocuous shells. Paragraphs suffice for the war on the Western Front and the Russian Front. No mention of the current fighting in Gallipoli.

With phrases from the four-month-old Gallipoli story comfortingly resounding in his ears—'absolute contempt of death', 'innumerable deeds of heroism', 'a display of the utmost gallantry', 'the bulldog breed'—the reader could relax. The leader writer drags a moral from the thunderstorms currently spoiling August holidays ('You dislike thunder exceedingly? It *is* a tiresome form of continuous occupation for the Forces'). The gossip columnist wonders how Lord Kitchener is standing the strain of the war and declares that 'the New Armies adore him, and there is not a soldier in the ranks who does not speak of him as "Kitch" or "Our Kitchy" '. The correspondence column gives pride of place to 'A Flapper' ('Because we like to give the "Tommies" and "Reggies" a little cheerful company, we are told that we are selfish and called "flirts" by people who do not look upon life in the same way as a happy-natured, happy-hearted girl does'). There is another 'splendid instalment' of Ruby M. Ayres's 'Her Way and His' ('There's no erring twice in Love and War'). A full-page advertisement, guaranteeing that SARGOL will 'increase your weight, round out your figure and make you shapely, popular and attractive', portrays a couple in bathing-costumes on a beach (remote indeed from Gallipoli) whispering about another couple: 'Look at that pair of skinny scarecrows. Why don't they try SAR-GOL.'

It was to this cosily blinkered world that Drewry returned on leave to England, after an absence of two years, to receive the VC from the hands of King George V at Buckingham Palace. And it is scarcely surprising to learn from Ralph Drewry that his brother confided little more to his family about his experiences than they had already read about. 'It was about the bravery of others that he talked. He said he was only doing his duty and had never expected the VC. When I showed him all the newspaper cuttings about him that we had kept he told me to put them in the toilet.'

Drewry's last three letters from Gallipoli describe the part he played in the landings at Suvla Bay on 7 August, when 20,000 fresh troops were poured ashore in an attempt to end the stalemate. Though a disjointed and confusing account, it indicates that the gallantry he had displayed at Helles was no flash in the pan. But the war was to provide him with no further outlets for heroism. He met his death, only three months before the end of the war, in a manner scarcely becoming to a national hero. Newspaper obituaries briefly record that he was accidentally killed at sea in northern waters when a block from the end of a derrick struck him heavily on the head.

Like most of the Great War's 634 VCs, Drewry's name might have faded into obscurity had it not been for a unique prominence given to it at the Imperial War Museum. His photograph hangs beside one of Commander Unwin alongside a dramatic tableau of the *River Clyde* landing, with model soldiers swarming down her gangways and leaping ashore from pinnaces under murderous shellfire, indicated by white splashes in a sea stained crimson at its verge. Two tiny figures in naval uniform, waist-deep in the sea as they strain at a line from the leading lighter, represent Unwin and Drewry.

The tableau is a focal point for many of the museum's 600,000 or more annual visitors. And listening to their comments is to be reminded of the transcience of fame, the levelling hand of history. Few have ever heard of the 'immortal story' of the *River Clyde*, fewer still of Drewry and his fellow-VCs.

'What they called landing craft in the first war, I suppose,' suggests a middle-aged man to his wife. 'Seem to have had a terrible time getting ashore,' she comments, peering briefly in at the hurly-burly before moving on. 'It was the Turks we was fighting wasn't it?' a mother asks her teenage son. 'No' he emphatically replies, 'the Italians.' Few stop to read the account of the landing and the parts played by the five VCs.

Over 46,000 Allied lives had been lost in the Gallipoli campaign by the time the last troops were evacuated from the peninsula in January 1916. And of all the 'heroic actions' that marked its tragic course, none so caught the popular fancy at the time as the use made of an old tramp steamer, a collier, as a modern Trojan Horse. As Drewry's letter indicates, he played a leading part in converting the *River Clyde* into a troopship for over 2,000 men of the Royal Munster Fusiliers and the Hampshire Regiment who packed her holds as, bristling with machine-guns behind her sandbagged bows, she made full steam ahead for that misty dawn-lit shore.

'V' beach, near the tip of the peninsula, was a natural amphitheatre, bounded to the north by the sheer slopes of Cape Helles, to the south by the ruined fort of Sedd-el-Bahr, with its village behind, the ground in between sloping towards a ridge. The plan was for an initial assault by Royal Dublin Fusiliers, leaping ashore from a flotilla of ships' boats, to be followed up by the surprise emergence of the troops from the *River Clyde*. Everything depended on the successful creation of a bridge between the grounded ship and the beach with the three lighters that had been towed alongside. A steam hopper had been assigned for this task. No one had foreseen that it would fail and that Commander Unwin would have to call upon his crew to manhandle the lighters into position. No one had foreseen that the Turks would be so formidably entrenched in the shelter of the ridge, holding their fire until the first boats touched shore.

Drewry's letter was written seventeen days after the landing and one wonders if an earlier letter would have had a less detached air about it. Only occasionally does emotion show through the recital of events, as when he describes the moment when the *River Clyde* began its dash towards the shore as the massed Fleet opened up a shattering bombardment ('Dad it was glorious!'). Excitement rather than fear underlies his account. One can imagine it written up into the climax to a blood-stirring boys' adventure story.

Drewry came third in a family of four brothers, the elder two now serving in the Royal Navy and the Merchant Service. His father, trained at sea, was a manager with the P & O company and had brought them up in a comfortable detached house in

Forest Gate, London. George was following in his steps when he left the Merchant Taylors' School, Blackheath, at the age of fourteen, to become an apprentice on the sailing ship *Indian Empire*. During the next three years he had voyaged to most parts of the world before joining the P & O service as an officer, plying to Australia and Japan.

The coolness and endurance he was to display at Gallipoli no doubt had their roots in this tough and sometimes perilous initiation. Newspaper cuttings mention an occasion when he fell from the mast of the *Indian Empire* into the sea and was nearly drowned before being rescued by the mate, and another when his ship was wrecked on an uninhabited island off Cape Horn and the crew were marooned for fourteen days before being rescued by a Chilean gunboat.

Both by background and bearing he was eminently cut out to figure as a popular hero. To Ralph Drewry he was a different kind of hero altogether. He still talks with emotion of the brother who was his only close companion in childhood and whose death he has never ceased to mourn.

Ralph Drewry became permanently deaf after an attack of scarlet fever at the age of four, and it was George, three years older than he, who made him feel that his disability need be no barrier to a normal life. He encouraged the lip-reading and sign language he learned at a school for the deaf, and today Mr Drewry can look back on a satisfying career as a boilermaker (he helped build invasion barges in the last war) and a happy married life. He is well able to communicate through lip-reading and the occasional written question.

'George was wonderful to me, we were always together as boys, like twins,' he recalls. 'I often think of those days. My earliest memory is of when we were small children playing in Wanstead Park and we stepped into a bog. We sank and sank, right up to our necks, until a passer-by heard our cries and hauled us out. I remember my father gave the man a new suit. I suppose if it hadn't been for him we would have drowned.'

Page 67   'Old Bill': the famous World War I cartoon character created by
Bruce Bairnsfather

Page 68   (above) Gallipoli: contemporary painting showing the landings from the *River Clyde*; (below) Kut: army surgeons operating in a field ambulance

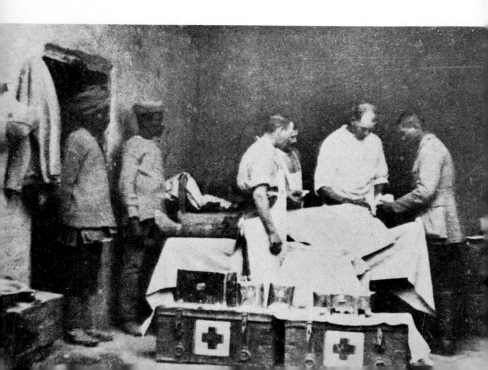

Mr Drewry is talking in his flat in a quiet road near the sea at Worthing, where he has lived alone since his wife died in 1970. On the sideboard there is a framed photograph of George among those of his two sons and two grandchildren and a copy of the oil painting he made of the *River Clyde*, now on permanent display at the Merchant Taylor's School together with George's VC. Mr Drewry has kept the Sword of Honour George was presented with by the Imperial Merchant Service Guild at a ceremony at Liverpool Town Hall and the faded snapshots he took from the beach the day after the landing, with bullets still flying around. But most of all he prizes the four letters George wrote to their father and the one to him which ends, 'Best of love, Dearest of Brothers'.

Copies of the letters are now among the rarer documents in the Imperial War Museum's archives. They may never have come to light had it not been for a chance visit made to the museum by Mr Drewry's eldest son in 1972. He told his father of that dramatic tableau of the *River Clyde* landing, and of the photograph of Midshipman Drewry beside it. Mr Drewry had been unaware of its existence, and until then had regarded his brother's letters of so long ago as of little more than family interest.

The first letter, in a bold copperplate hand, was written aboard the *River Clyde*, still grounded off 'V' beach, with a battle of the trenches now raging a short distance inland and the fleet still under shellfire.

HMS *River Clyde*
Sedd-el-Bahr
Turkey
12 May 1915

'Dearest Father, I'm awfully afraid I've made you anxious by missing the last two mails, I did write a letter on the 21st of April but tore it up again. In my last letter I think I told you that two RN midshipmen were joining the *Hussar* to help me.

Well they came, and we worked in three watches for two days until I got tired of doing nothing so asked the Captain [Unwin] for more work, well I got it with a vengeance.

'He took me on board this ship and gave me thirty Greeks and told me to clean her. Well she was the dirtiest ship I've seen. She was in ballast and had just brought French mules up from Algiers, they had built boxes and floors in the tween-decks and carried the mules there without worrying about sanitary arrangements.

'We knocked the boxes up and cleaned her up for troops, painted the starboard side P & O colour. A large square port was cut on each side of each hatch in the tween-decks and from the No 2 ports I rigged stages right round the bow. A party of the armoured car people came on board and rigged small huts of plates and sandbags and put maxims in them, 11 altogether. After two days' delay on account of weather we put to sea on the 23rd April at 1 pm towing three lighters and a steamboat alongside (port) and a steam hopper on the starboard side. As soon as we cleared the shipping we dropped the lighters astern.

'Now I will tell you of our crew. Capt: Comdr. Unwin, RN (retired supplementary), 1st Lieut: Mid. Drewry, RNR and Warrant Eng. Horend, RNR, nine seamen and nine stokers, one carpenter's mate, the original ship's steward and the Captain's servant. [The two VC seamen were Williams and Samson, mentioned later.] Can you imagine how proud I felt as we steamed down the line, I on the fo'c's'le-head. The flag-ship (no longer *Hussar*) wished us luck as we passed. As soon as the tow was dropped I took the bridge until the Capt had lunch then I had mine and carried on with the work for there were many things to be done. At dusk we anchored off Tenedos and that night we had pheasant for dinner, a present from the captain of the *Soudan*.

'Next morning things looked bad, a nasty breeze made us afraid our show would not come off, but it died quickly.

About 6 am a signal came to us telling us we were in some-one's berth so we had to weigh and for an hour we wandered among the ships with our long tail just scraping along ships' sides and across their bows. We were nobody's dog, nobody loved us. Finally we tied up to the stern of the *Fawcette* and we put the last touches to the staging on the bow. About 4 pm the sweepers came alongside with the troops. At 11.30 pm all was ready and the Capt told me to snatch some sleep. At midnight we proceeded in this fashion [sketch of ship with vessels in tow].

'At 2 am or thereabouts the Capt turned over to me, and I found myself on the bridge very sleepy with only the helmsman, steering towards the Turkish searchlights on a calm night, just making headway against the current, shadowy forms of des-troyers and battleships slipping past me. Visions of mines and submarines rose before me as I thought of the $2\frac{1}{2}$ thousand men in the holds and I felt very young. Between 3 and 4 am the Capt took over again and I went to sleep again being called at 5 am, "Captain says you are to take over the hopper." So I climbed over the side across the lighters into the hopper.

'Then came an anxious time, we steered straight toward Cape Helles and in a few minutes the bombardment commenced, Dad it was glorious! Dozens of ships, battleships, cruisers, des-troyers and transports. The morning mist lay on the land, which seemed to be a mass of fire and smoke as the ships raked it with their 12 inch, the noise was awful and the air full of powder. Shells began to fall round us thick but did not hit us. We were half a mile from the beach and we were told not yet, so we took a turn round two ships, at last we had the signal at 6 am and in we dashed, Unwin on the bridge and I at the helm of the hopper with my crew of six Greeks and one sailor Samson.

'At 6.10 the ship struck, very easily she brought up, and I shot ahead and grounded on her port bow. Then the fun began, picket boats towed lifeboats full of soldiers inshore and slipped them as the water shoaled and they rowed the rest of the way, the soldiers jumped out as the boats beached and they died, almost all of them wiped out with the boats' crews. We had a line from the stern of the hopper to the lighters and this we tried to haul in, the hardest haul I've ever tried. Then the Capt appeared on the lighters and the steam pinnace took hold of the lighters and plucked them in until she could go no closer. Instead of joining up to the hopper the Capt decided to make the connection with a spit of rock on the other bow.

'Seeing this we let go our rope and Samson and I tried to put a brow out over the bow, the Greeks had run below and two of us could not do it, so I told him also to get out of the rain of bullets, and I jumped over the bow and waded ashore, meeting a soldier wounded in the water. I and another soldier from a boat tried to carry him ashore but he was again shot in our arms, his neck in two pieces nearly, so we left him and I ran along the beach towards the spit. I threw away my revolver, coat and hat and waded out to the Captain, he was in the water with a man named Williams wading and towing the lighters towards the spit. I gave a pull for a few minutes and then climbed aboard the lighters and got the brows lowered onto the lighter. The Capt still in the water sang out for more rope, so I went onboard and brought a rope down with the help of a man called Ellard. As we reached the end of the lighters the Capt was wading towards us carrying Williams. We pulled him onto the lighters and Ellard carried him onboard the ship on his shoulders, but he spoilt the act by not coming down again. Williams was dead however.

'I got a rope from the lighter to the spit and then with difficulty I hauled the Capt onto the lighter, he was nearly done and I was alone. He went inboard and the doctor had rather a job with him. All the time shells were falling all round us and into the ship one hitting the casing of one boiler but doing no further damage. Several men were killed in No 4 hold. I stayed on the lighters and tried to keep the men going ashore but it was murder and soon the first lighter was covered with dead and wounded and the spit was awful, the sea round it for some yards was red. When they got ashore they were little better off for they were picked off many of them before they could dig themselves in.

'They stopped coming and I ran onboard into No 1 hold and saw an awful sight, dead and dying lay around the ports where their curiosity had led them. I went up to the saloon and saw the Capt being rubbed down, he murmured something about the third lighter so I went down again and in a few minutes a picket boat came along the starboard side and gave the reserve lighter a push that sent it as far as the hopper (the lighters had drifted away from the spit) with Lieut Morse and myself on it. Just as we hit the hopper a piece of shrapnel hit me on the head knocking me down for a second or two and covering me with blood. However we made the lighter fast to the hopper and then I went below in the hopper and a Tommy put my scarf round my head and I went up again.

'Now we wanted a connection to the other lighters so I took a rope and swam towards the other lighters but the rope was not long enough and I was stuck in the middle. I sang out to Mid Malleson [the other Midshipman VC] who had arrived with Morse in the picket boat, to throw me a line but he had no line except the one that had originally kept the lighters to the spit, he stood up and hauled this line in (almost half a coil) and then, as I had drifted away, he swam towards the lighter I had left and made it alright. Then I made for home but had a job climbing up the lighters for I was rather played out.

'When I got onboard the doctor dressed my head and rubbed me down, I was awfully cold. He would not let me get up and I had to lay down and listen to the din. Then I heard a cheer and looking out of the port I saw the Capt standing on the hopper in white clothes, a line had carried away and by himself he had fixed it. Then I went to sleep and woke at 3 pm to find the hopper's bow had swung round and there was no connection with the shore. I got up and found that nothing was going to be done until dark. At dusk the firing seemed to cease, and the connection was made to the spit again.

'During the time I was asleep the Captain and one or two volunteers had taken seven loads of wounded from the lighters to No 4 hold by the starboard side. A great feat which everyone is talking about. About 8 pm the troops commenced to land again and things went well as far as firing goes. While the troops were going out I had a party getting wounded from the hopper and lighters and putting them onboard a trawler lying under our quarter. An awful job, they had not been dressed at all and some of the poor devils were in an awful state, I never knew blood smelt so strong before.

'About 11.30 pm the trawler had left and almost all the troops were ashore and the Turks gave us an awful doing, shell, shrapnel and every other nasty thing, but everyone lay low and little harm was done. They finished about 2 am. All through the night the village was burning and gave us too much light to be pleasant.

'Next day was not pleasant, early in the morning our people worked up the right and took the fort and then worked slowly into the village and took it house by house. Then Col Doughty-Wylie led a charge up the ridge and was killed just as he led his men into the old fort on top of the ridge. All this we saw plainly from the ship. I had a run ashore across the spit and took a photo from the beach but the bullets began to fly so I ran back. It was not until the next day that all the snipers were cleared from the ridge and village.

'Samson my hopper man did very well on the Sunday afternoon, two or three times he took wounded from the beach to the hopper. On the second day he was severely wounded while sniping from the fore deck. Nothing much happened that night except that a dog frightened one Tommy, he fired at it and so did the rest for nearly an hour.

'I won't follow up the soldiers or the censor would tear this up, ten minutes walk and I can see the men in the trenches, in

74

the straits I can see the enemy's shells falling round our ships and always the roar of guns goes on. We have been bombarded by aeroplanes but no damage done. I've seen a German chased by two of our planes.

'My Capt has just left us for another job and soon I expect to be back to the *Hussar* again. By next mail I hope to send you some photos taken here, some of them I believe will be of interest and I'm wondering if you could send them to the papers for me.

'The Admiral sent for me on the 28th and gave me a shift of clean clothes and the use of his bath, some luck.

'There is lots yet I could tell you but I must not so will send my love and close.

Best of health,

Your affectionate Son,

George

'NB   Have just received yours of the 15th and 22nd, glad you are keeping so well.'

Some time later Drewry's parents received a letter they must have long cherished from Dr R. Burrowes Kelly, RN, the Fleet Surgeon aboard the *River Clyde*. He received the DSO, the citation telling how, though wounded in the foot on the morning of 25 April, he had remained at his post till the morning of the 27th, attending to 750 wounded during that time although himself in great pain and unable to walk. His is the burly, grim-faced figure seated next to Drewry in that photograph taken on the beach.

'I am taking the liberty of writing to you just a few lines about your most gallant of sons, our beloved midshipman who has made himself and incidentally all those with him famous. I maintain that I am the only person living who can ever know what Commander Unwin and your son did on April 25th both before and after they were knocked out. Why both were not killed I cannot tell you and one must look to some one higher for the reason, God alone can know. I saw them flushed with victory, faced with defeat and death and so on turn about. When the Commander lay in a dangerous condition your son took over sole charge, when your son was finished Commander Unwin was ready although unfit to relieve him.

'George has a tremendous future in front of him, because his fame will not affect him but only tend to elevate him still higher. His absolute contempt of death, love of duty and modesty were proverbial amongst us all both military and naval. You must indeed be proud of this splendid fellow and that he will be spared for many years to gladden your hearts is my one wish.

'To have been with such a body of naval men has been a great honour indeed, and I shall never forget that I was their doctor who did what little I could for them all. All were great but *River Clyde* Drewry as he is now known was the greatest. He and Samson the leading Seaman have borne out Nelson's old dictum "My guns may change, my ships may change, but the spirit of my men remains."

'Trusting you will pardon this intrusion on my part and again asking you to accept my warmest congratulations on being the parents of such a son,

Believe me,
Yours very sincerely,
R. Burrowes Kelly
Surgeon'

4　*Gallipoli Survivor*

On 1 May 1915, under shellfire in a newly dug trench near the tip of the Gallipoli peninsula, Captain Guy Warneford Nightingale sat among the remnants of his company of Royal Munster Fusiliers writing a letter to his mother about the part he had played in one of the bloodiest and most hazardous assaults of the war. Five days before he had been among the few officers to survive the murderous hail of Turkish bullets that met the troops storming ashore from their floating Trojan Horse, the converted collier *River Clyde*. And of the savage fighting that had followed, and was still in progress, he was able to write: 'I have had some extraordinary escapes but haven't been touched yet.'

Throughout the Gallipoli campaign Nightingale maintained his early reputation of 'bearing a charmed life', and in his eighteen letters home his descriptions of the horrors of trench warfare, during which he not infrequently saw men shot dead at his side, display a remarkable stoicism. 'I've had bullets through all parts of my clothing and two bayonet thrusts—one through my glasses and another through my belt!' is a typically buoyant observation.

Nightingale was a regular, steeped in the traditions of a regiment with a long history of service to the British Raj, and there is a professional tone to his letters that seems to accept the

77

The landings at Gallipoli

war, even in its most fearful aspects, as a stepping-stone in his career. He has little time for the territorial and militia officers brought in to replace the killed or wounded regulars—'extra-ordinarily helpless, frightfully keen and about as much idea of soldiering as the Man in the Moon'. A strong sense of esprit de corps is countered by an uncompromisingly bloodthirsty atti-tude to the enemy. 'All the streams were running blood,' he tells his sister in one letter, 'and the heaps of dead were a grand sight.'

It was in 1972 that Nightingale's sister, Mrs Margaret (Meta) Warneford Hesketh-Williams, a widow in her eighty-fourth year whose memory was failing, sought to perpetuate the memory of her dead brother by presenting photostat copies of his Gallipoli letters to the Public Record Office, who passed them on to the Imperial War Museum as being of 'considerable historical interest'. Today Mrs Hesketh-Williams lives in an old people's home, no longer able to communicate, and it was her daughter, Mrs C. M. F. Coleman, who shed a totally un-expected light on the writer of these chilling letters, her un-known uncle.

The immediate impression one gets from reading Nightingale's letters is of an extrovert man of action, self-reliant and resource-ful, taking life—and death—in his stride. But knowledge of even the few facts that can be gleaned about him indicates that this is an inadequate assessment, that the stiff upper lip knew how to tremble. Nightingale's letters, mostly written to his mother, take on a new dimension of poignancy when one learns that he had passed most of his childhood deprived of parental love and that he died, in 1935, a bachelor recluse, by his own hand.

Nightingale's father, married for the second time and with a family by his first wife, was Chief Engineer in the Public Works Department in India and at an early age Guy and his sister, Meta, who was a year older, were sent to England to be educated. Mrs Coleman has gathered from her mother that they were brought up by kindly foster-parents, friends of the family, and suffered none of the traumatic miseries recounted by Rudyard Kipling in a similar childhood exile from his parents in India. But she wonders if this deprivation might have been partially responsible for the fits of depression to which both were subject in later life. She met her Uncle Guy only once, when she was eight, but can recall nothing about him. The impression she got was that he had 'made nothing of his life' after the war, and that his mother, a dominant personality, regarded him as 'weak'.

Nightingale started prep school at the age of five, went on to Rugby (in one letter he refers to an officer who was 'in the Bug's house at Rugby with me') and thence to Sandhurst. The first record of his Army career, in the official history of the Royal Munster Fusiliers, is of his appointment as 2nd lieutenant in 1910, at the age of twenty. The regiment (dissolved in 1922) was created in 1756, boasted Robert Clive as its first colonel and had numerous battle honours ranging from the battle of Plassey to the Boer War. And to dip into that two-volume history is to get a revealing glimpse of the tradition-bound blinkered world in which, as his letters suggest, Nightingale found the security of a substitute home.

At the time he joined the regiment it was engaged in sporadic skirmishes with hostile tribes on the North West Frontier of India (where his grandfather had once served as a padre). Here, and later in Burma, the history records such events in much the same way as it records the prowess of teams in inter-regimental hockey, boxing, tug-of-war and bayonet fighting contests (it is significant that in one letter Nightingale equates the killing of Turks with big game shooting). There is a public school heartiness about it all which even echoes, like the rallying cry to a sporting field, in the message delivered to the Fusiliers

Brigade by its commanding officer on the eve of the Gallipoli landings: 'Our task will be no easy one. Let us carry it through in such a way that the men of Albuhera, Minden, Delhi and Lucknow may hail us as their equal in valour and military achievements, and that future historians may say of us as Napier said of the Fusilier Brigade at Albuhera: "Nothing could stop this astonishing infantry." '

The landings, particularly at 'V' beach in the shadow of Cape Helles, were to be even less of an easy task than had been envisaged, and in the ensuing fighting nothing went according to plan. Controversy has raged over the stalemate of trench warfare that developed and led to a futile slaughter for much of the eight months of the campaign, and Nightingale's letters are illuminating in giving the on-the-spot (and surprisingly uncensored) judgements of an officer in the thick of it all.

He is proud to belong to the 'astonishing infantry' that nothing could stop, quoting captured German officers as saying that 'no army in the world except ours could have seen half its numbers mown down and still come on and make good a landing', and puts all the blame for lost opportunities on the 'people in authority'. 'If we had only had enough troops in the beginning to keep them on the run we would have had the whole peninsula by now', he writes two weeks after the landing. Two weeks later he writes: 'The whole thing has been thoroughly mismanaged . . . There's one thing quite certain—we can't get off the peninsula now we are on', (in the event, the gradual and furtive withdrawal of 115,000 men from under the noses of the Turks was the only operation that went triumphantly to plan).

It is scarcely surprising that the Gallipoli campaign has been so frequently written about. Its very setting, across the waters of the Dardanelles (the ancient Hellespont) from the plains of Homer's Troy, gives an almost legendary dimension to a conflict that might have been presided over by malignant gods (of the elements as well as of war) rather than by bungling generals. From warships and transports cruising along its coastline, the spectator focusing his glasses on its bare and sun-scorched hills and plains might have been peering into some nightmare arena of subterranean combat.

Reading Nightingale's letters from the beach-head one is aware of those watching eyes, as though a curtain was rising, a tragedy beginning to unfold. Aboard the *Queen Elizabeth*, the most powerful battleship afloat, General Sir Ian Hamilton, Commander-in-Chief of the land forces, and his staff were horrified witnesses of the carnage on 'V' beach. Next day, as Midshipman Drewry's letter testifies, the watchers followed with baited breath the capture by the Munster and Dublin Fusiliers of the castle and village of Sedd-el-Bahr and the bayonet charge up the ridge beyond. No doubt Drewry glimpsed for an instant the figure of Captain Nightingale beside that of Colonel Doughty-Wylie, the staff officer aboard the *River Clyde* who had gone ashore to rally the almost leaderless troops and lead the attack. As Nightingale's first letter indicates, the valiant colonel, later awarded a posthumous VC, was at his side when he was shot dead as they crested the ridge.

Nightingale was twice mentioned in despatches in Gallipoli, was later awarded the MC and made a Chevalier of the Legion d'Honneur on the Western Front. Of his courage there can be no doubt, and it is difficult to detect in these letters any sign of the weakness of character his mother was later in life to deplore. Mrs Coleman pictures her grandmother at the time as the kind of patriot who would have 'applauded the white feather ladies', and it is evident from her son's letters that she took a close interest in his army career and was acquainted with many of the officers in his regiment. His few references to letters received from her give no indication as to how far she sought to sustain him through the ordeal. Apart from one suggestive sentence—'You weren't far wrong when you thought we would have a tough job landing on the peninsula'—they are mainly concerned with parcels from home.

Is there between the lines of these letters something of a pose, a desire to impress, or even an inarticulate cry for the motherly love that had been denied him in childhood? Or does the resilience they portray indicate that in the heat of battle he found himself in his element, sustained by the comradeship of brother officers, life stripped to fundamentals and freed of personal cares? 'Lots of fellows are going off their heads out here but personally I've never felt better in my life, I eat and sleep like a pig and feel most awfully cheerful', he writes in a letter to his sister six weeks after the landing, and it sounds like more than a younger brother's bravado.

Meta was serving as a VAD nurse, with digs in Lambeth, at the time, and their parents (the date of their return from India is not known) were living at Bushey Park, Hertfordshire. Of the eighteen typescript copies of the letters (the originals have not been traced) three long ones are to his sister, one shorter one to his father. In parts there is an overlapping of events described and in the extracts that follow I have chosen the more vivid account (Nightingale's letters to his sister have a slightly more relaxed, debonair tone to them).

'*1 May*. Dear Mother, This is the first opportunity I have had of writing to you since we left the boat. You will have seen the papers by now, that we have forced a landing, but ourselves and the Dublins got most awfully mauled in doing so. We left Lemnos for Tenedos one day, and from there we got a collier called the *River Clyde*, which had been fitted up for the purpose of beaching. We anchored at midnight about two miles from the mouth of the Dardanelles, and at dawn the whole Fleet began a bombardment of the end of the peninsula where we were going to land.

'At 7.30 am the Dublins set off in open boats to their landing place which was the same as ours. As each boat got near the shore, snipers shot down the oarsmen. The boats began to drift, and machine-gun fire was turned on to them. You could see the men dropping everywhere, and of the first boatload of 40 men only 3 reached the shore, all wounded. At the same time we ran the old collier on to the shore but the water was shallower than they thought and she stuck about 80 yards out. Some lighters were put to connect with the shore and we began running along them to get down to the beach. I can't tell you how many were killed or drowned but the place was a regular death-trap.

'I ran down to the lighters but was sent back by Jarrett as there was no room on them. Then the wounded began crawling back, the Turks sniping at them the whole time. The men who had managed to reach the shore were all crouching under a bank about 10 feet high, among them Jarrett. At 2 pm the Colonel told me to go down on to the barge, collect as many men as I could and join the force on shore. We jumped into the sea and got ashore somehow with a rain of bullets all round us. I found Jarrett and a lot of men but very few not hit. We waited till dusk and then crept up into a sort of position a few yards up. We took up an outpost line and I had just put up my sentry groups and Jarrett came up to have a look, when he was shot through the throat by my side. He died very soon and that left me the Senior Officer on shore.'

[Continued from letter to Meta] 'We dug ourselves in, the Turks sniping at us from every corner and I've never spent such a rotten night. It was pouring with rain too. During the night all the rest of the regt landed and by the morning we had what remained of us, one company of the Dublins and one company of the Hants under Major Beckwith. We were told to take an old ruined castle, full of Turks, then a village and finally storm a hill with a redoubt at the top. The castle was rushed at the point of the bayonet and we lost only a few. The village was an awful snag. Every house and corner was full of snipers and you only had to show yourself in the streets to have a bullet at your head. We spent from 9 am to 2.30 before we finally cleared them all out, we lost a lot of men and officers in it. I got one swine of a Turk with my revolver when searching a house for snipers but he nearly had me first.

'By 3 we held a line at the far end of the village and the hill
we had to take was immediately above us. The *Queen Elizabeth*
and 4 other Men-of-War then shelled the hill and at 4.30 we
were ordered to fix bayonets and take the hill. My company
led the attack with the Dubliners and we had a great time. We
saw the enemy, which was the chief thing, and the men all
shouted and enjoyed it tremendously. It *was* a relief after all
that appalling sniping. We rushed straight to the top and turned
2,000 Turks off the redoubt and poured lead into them at about
10 yards range. Colonel Doughty-Wylie who led the whole
attack was killed at my side. I wrote in about him to the Staff
and he has been recommended for the VC. I buried him that
evening and got our padre to read the service over him. It was
6 by the time we finished firing on the Turks and we dug ourselves in in an outpost position.'

[Letter to Mother continued] 'That night we were attacked
at intervals all through but held our own till 1,000 French troops
reinforced us. The next day we were moved up and dug ourselves in again while two other brigades advanced a mile. The
next morning we were told to move up to the advanced line and
act in reserve, but by the time we got up to it the firing line was
so hard pressed that we had to go straight up into it. We had a
very heavy day's fighting being under fire continuously from
8 am till dark. The next morning we advanced about 100 yards
in and the whole Division dug itself in in a long line across the
peninsula from sea to sea. We are still holding this line and
have got three and a half miles of the peninsula now. We get
shelled all day, and sniped at and attacked all night, but are
very cheery. We have plenty of food now and water and have
dug ourselves into the ground like in France . . .

'The German officers whom we have taken prisoner say it is
absolutely beyond them how we ever effected a landing at all.
If there was one place in the whole world that was impregnable
it was this peninsula and they say no army in the world except
ours could have seen half its numbers mown down and still

come on and make good a landing. It has certainly been a tough job. The heaps of dead are awful and the beach where we landed was an extraordinary sight the morning they buried them. I buried Major Jarrett just before dawn and have his few personal belongings which I hope to be able to send to his people soon. I have had some extraordinary escapes but haven't been touched yet . . .'

[Further extract from letter to Meta] 'On the night of the first of May we had a tremendous attack. They crept up in the dark and were in our trenches and bayonetting our men before we knew the attack had begun. We lost some trenches but recovered them all in half an hour . . . The attack went on from 10.30 pm till dawn. The Turks attacked again and again shouting "Allah! Allah!". It was most exciting hearing them collecting in a dip in the hill about 40 yards away waiting for their next charge. We mowed them down and only once did they get so close that we were able to bayonet them. When dawn broke, we saw them in hundreds retiring and simply mowed them down. We took 300 prisoners and could have taken 3,000 but we preferred shooting them. All the streams were simply running blood and the heaps of dead were a grand sight . . .'

'*10 May*. Dear Mother, Here we are, back again after 15 days continuous fighting. I wrote a few days ago, but a mail goes in a few minutes, so I will not miss this opportunity of writing. Also I have a letter from you received this morning in answer to mine from Alex. I am glad you liked the photos.

'We had a bad time the day before yesterday. Just at 5 in the evening we were ordered to advance 800 yards and dig in. We were in the most advanced line. Williams and I were leading our coy and Waldegrave came in with half of his, while the remainder were in support. We only got 200 yards and in that distance in a couple of minutes my coy lost 7 killed and 23 wounded. Poor Waldegrave was badly hit next to me. He was hit practically through the heart and then through both lungs.

We had to dig in then and there under heavy fire and only 400 yards from a Turkish redoubt which was sweeping the whole ground with machine-gun fire. We made some sort of a line and hung on all night expecting to be attacked, but the Turks got such a bad knock in the last night attack they think twice now. Williams and I both escaped being hit luckily though how anyone escaped is a marvel to me.

'The next day we were supported by some Australians and New Zealanders. We hung on all day and were then relieved by the Worcesters. We were ordered back two miles to the left in the firing-line and with two coys of the KOS Borderers were ordered to make a night attack and entrench in a position 500 yards in front. Two regiments had already been wiped out trying to do it in daylight. We advanced 300 strong and 3 officers at 1 am. When we reached the place we were heard by the Turks and they opened up a heavy fire on us. It was pitch dark. A fortnight before two regiments had attempted to force a landing there and after fighting for 16 hours had to re-embark, leaving about 700 of their own dead and about 1,500 Turks. These bodies were still lying there highly decomposed and the stench was awful. In the dark we kept tumbling over the bodies and treading on them. When it was light I found that I had dug in next to the remains of an officer in the KOSB whom I had last seen at the opera at Malta and had spent a most jolly evening with. There were ten KOSBs and seven South Wales Borderers officers lying there but I only recognised a few.

'We found we could not hold on as we were enfiladed so had to retire back to the entrenchments. In the morning a subaltern in the Dublins and myself went to do a recce. We crept half a mile round the cliff and got to within a few yards of some Turkish trenches. We could hear them talking and saw them cooking. It was most tantalising not being able to shoot. There were about 7,000 of them. We went back, after sketching the position, to bring up the regiment. I led up the Dublins and just as we got 200 men up there the Turks opened a cross-fire

87

on us from two machine-guns. They had had them the whole
time and we must have got very close to them when we crept
up to sketch the position. Out of the first six men up there I was
the only one not hit. It was no good stopping there. If the men
had been fresh and not absolutely exhausted we might have
rushed the machine-gun with the bayonet but it was quite out
of the question.

'I dressed up the two worst wounded men and we all got
back under cover on the beach. I had an extraordinary escape.
A bullet missed me by about an 8th of an inch and went
straight into the throat of a man sitting next to me. We got
back without further difficulties and the men were too tired to
do anything else. As a matter of fact, we were going back anyway to the base for a rest, so we just had 2 hours rest and then
moved back to the beach. We had had no rations for 48 hours
and no sleep for 3 days, so you can imagine how glad we were
to find a space allotted to us on the sand and told to draw
rations and then eat and sleep as much as we wanted. The first
thing I did was to have a bathe in the sea and not having taken
off any of my clothes for over a week, and before that only my
socks, it was the most refreshing bath I've ever had . . .

'Our RC padre is a splendid fellow, he is always right up in
the trenches with us and does a wonderful lot of good. I go to
Mass whenever our padre holds it in the trenches or in camp.
This is now degenerating into a kind of trench warfare. We
can't possibly advance, nor can the Turks. If we had only had
enough troops in the beginning to keep them on the run we
would have the whole peninsula by now. I have had my head
clipped all over with the horse-clippers, so I must get someone
to photograph me and send you a copy! . . .'

'*10 May* . . . I am looking forward to seeing the papers describing out landing and subsequent movements very much,
but I expect it will be a long time before anything like a detailed
account will be given. I see the casualties are being spread over
several days in order to break it gently to the good people at

home . . . We four officer survivors curiously enough are the four who represented the battalion at the bomb-throwing course at Rugby! We all have the reputation of bearing charmed lives, I don't know really how we escaped. I've had bullets through all parts of my clothing and two bayonet thrusts—one through my glasses and another through my belt!

'You will be glad to hear that I was mentioned in General Hunter-Weston's despatches for the night attack of May 1st and recommended for anything that was going as a fellow called O'Hara and myself organised a counter-attack and re-took some trenches temporarily occupied by the Turks when they rushed us in the dark. As a matter of fact it was the most natural thing to do and the Turks didn't wait long for us when they saw we meant to retake the trenches. I don't like fighting in the dark at all. It is so easy to be killed by one's own men . . .

'We bathe all day long (with spent bullets falling among us in a most cheerful manner) and it is most refreshing. I have worn the sulphur bag all along and have certainly been free from all wild animals! I look on it as a mascot too! We had a bull terrier presented to the Battalion by the Coventry people as a mascot and he came here with us, and is now living on the battleship *Agamemnon* where he is being treated much better than any of the wounded! . . .

'I was told today that the Malta *Gazette* of May 4th had an account of our landing and also some of the chief casualties such as General Napier and General Hare. I saw General Napier killed. He went down the gangway just in front of me followed by Brigade Major Costello. He was hit in the stomach on the barge between our ship and the beach. He lay for half an hour on the barge and then tried to get some water to drink but the moment he moved the Turks began firing at him again and whether he was hit again or not I do not know, but he died very soon afterwards, and when I went ashore for the second time I turned him over and he was quite dead . . .'

'*14 May* [to his father] . . . Yesterday morning I had to go

on board the *Dublin,* one of our newest cruisers out here. She
was going to shell some Turkish trenches which we had been
opposite. I had to crawl out and find out who they faced and
where they were exactly, so I was sent for to explain exactly to
the *Dublin.* I had to climb to the masthead up the rigging, which
alarmed me a lot, but you get a fine view from there. After
pointing out all I knew, we adjourned for lunch, a magnificent
meal to me after living on bully beef and biscuits for nearly
three weeks! I also washed my hands in warm water for the
first time since I left the transport. I had a chop and nearly ate
a whole loaf of bread to my own cheek! I also had a bottle of
beer and a liqueur and they filled up my pockets with cigars
and chocolate to take back to our Mess. On the whole I spent a
very pleasant day. I had never before been on a cruiser when
she was cleared for action so it was all very interesting. We
were quite close to the *Queen Elizabeth.*

'This morning I was down on what we call beach "W"
where all the guns and stores and ammo is being landed and
they began shelling us. It was most critical at one time as they
dropped some heavy shells in the middle of the transport lines
and killed 50 horses and 29 men in a few minutes. The ammo
was piled up near to the transport, millions of rounds and shells
and if they had exploded it would have blown us all away.
They say the *Goeben*'s big 12 inch guns have landed and are
behind a hill called Achi Baba and it is they which are doing
all the damage.

'As I am writing there is a transport about a quarter of a mile
out from our beach getting shelled. She has just had 7 running
on her decks and unless she hurries up and gets a move on, she
will either be sunk or set on fire . . . A tremendous lot more
shells have burst on the old transport, but she is getting up
steam now. Major Hutchinson has just come along to say she is
full of wounded men and is the *Ajax,* a hospital ship. We are
getting a lot of our slightly wounded men back now. I see they
are breaking our casualties gently to you at home. Out of the

14 officers of ours hit on Sunday April 25 the *Times* of the 2nd May only gives Major Jarrett killed and five wounded. A lot of the regiments like the Lancs Fusiliers who lost 20 officers the first day are not mentioned at all! I think the Dublins are the only complete list. I suppose they'll try and make out it's been nothing at all out here, just a scrap with the Turks, whereas it's been hell and frightfully mismanaged. There are any number of officers and men here who have had five or six months in France and were right through Mons and they say it was nothing, a mere picnic, compared to the landing and subsequent 14 days of this show. We expect to get back to the firing-line tomorrow . . .'

'*22 May* [to Meta] RMS *Franconia* . . . I indulged in 6 days malaria and was finally sent on board here last night to recover, as there seemed to be no chance whatever of my getting rid of it where we were. The change here is extraordinary. I got on board about 9 pm last night, having come out in a destroyer (I'm at Mudus by the way in the *Archipelago*, about five hours from the peninsula) in company with one other officer and 143 wounded men. I had an egg, the first I've tasted for a month, and a BATH (*hot*) and then went to bed in SHEETS, and couldn't sleep a wink for the comfort of it all! This morning I woke up and shaved off my three weeks' beard and had another bath. I feel awfully rotten and weak from the fever but otherwise very well.

'This is a magnificent ship, with sitting-rooms and lounges and verandahs with ivy and creepers all over them and a gymnasium and all sorts of things on board. I have a palatial cabin to myself and there are hardly any people on board. It is only a convalescent ship, so one gets away from all the horrible cases one sees such a lot of on shore. It's really most peaceful. We can't even hear the heavy guns from here, and I am just beginning to feel again that life really is worth living when you once get away from nasty things like bullets and stray limbs and decomposed corpses.

'I saw a *Daily Telegraph* today of May 13th which had an account of our landing in it, but no names of regiments, so I sent it on home with some notes which might make it more interesting. If you would like to send something really useful and inexpensive I'd very much like a small looking-glass for shaving. The best are not made of glass but polished tin and go in a khaki case absolutely flat, about half the size of this sheet of paper. It would be very useful, at present if I do shave, which is seldom, I have to use the inside of my watch as a glass and it's highly unsatisfactory . . .'

'*24 May* [to his mother] RMS *Franconia* . . . The sun is beginning to get very hot here now and water becoming scarce though the RE are busy sinking wells and leading off streams. I've just read the *Water Babies* through again, it sounds very peaceful amongst all this hubbub. Yesterday there was a 12-hour armistice in the peninsula to bury the dead—a highly necessary action as the smell was becoming unbearable.

'There ought to be a mail waiting for us when I get back. I see they've brought in another half-dozen militia captains over our heads, it is the limit the way the War Office treat regular officers. I don't care whether I call myself captain or lieutenant but I do care whether I draw the extra pay of the higher rank and at this rate I'll never reach a captaincy if they continue to bring in these fellows.' [Three weeks later Nightingale learned from his mother of his promotion to captain, backdated to 24 February, 'which means over £100 back pay being credited to me!']

'*1 June.* Here we are back at old V Beach! We are resting after 3 days in the trenches. It is awfully nice here. I'm in a dugout with Williams. We look straight down 100 feet onto the beach, with the *River Clyde* at our feet and opposite us the old castle where Jarrett's grave is and Sedd-el-Bahr village, while behind are the plains of Troy, Mount Ida and Kum Kale Fort with glimpses of the Dardanelles separating us from the Asiatic side. Our camp is the fort here. The French are using the beach as a landing place and depot. It is so different now. Not a blade of grass left, only rows and rows of tents and horses with a great round patch of cornfields and poppies in the middle surrounded by barbed wire—the grave of 430 Dublins and Munsters and 14 officers of these two regiments who were killed at the landing on V Beach.

'We still get shelled here. "Slippery Sam", a well known gun from Achi Baba never fails to give us half a dozen high explosives morning and evening, while "Asiatic Annie", a most attentive howitzer from the Asiatic side of the Straits, is perpetually keeping us on the look-out and accounts for many horses daily. The old *River Clyde* is just the same, but now inhabited by two middies, a naval doctor who has been on since April 25th and the landing staff. We are often there and always greeted as the proper owners of her . . .

'We've just got orders about a big attack on Achi Baba which will probably end up in a kind of Neuve Chapelle for us. We are bound to lose very heavily but it's got to be done. We are expecting to move off any moment, and that is why I'am writing while I have the opportunity. We have now 38 officers! Geddes is commanding and with five of us originals and with 33 territorials and militia and special reserve people we are a most peculiar crowd. The new ones are very funny—extraordinary helpless, frightfully keen and about as much idea of soldiering as the Man in the Moon. There are no battleships here now owing to the submarines but we've got tons of guns ashore.

'The sun is just setting and all the beach is purple while the turrets and battlements of the castle just catch the last rays and the Dardanelles are deep blue under Mount Ida. The sunsets here are glorious—like during the rains in Rangoon. The only thing that spoils it is the incessant bombardment of heavy guns. There is a most noisy battery of guns of the French about $\frac{1}{4}$ mile from us, and they never cease firing and drawing Asiatic Annie's fire every day which is most unpleasant! However, we get some excellent claret from their Mess, which they get as a ration, and we swop for our cheese and jam which they don't get, so there are some uses for even French batteries . . .'

'Yesterday I went down to look at Jarrett's grave and took a party to build up a substantial wall all round. Afterwards I went over our old battlefield again and up through the village. Looking at it now I cannot understand how we ever got up here at all, and it beats me altogether why the Turks ever left their trenches. It seems ridiculous, looking at the positions now, that 2,000 Turks should ever have allowed themselves to have been turned out by 400 of us. I have done a rough sketch on this piece of paper from my dugout where I am sitting now. The place where I have written "bank under which we lay all day" is where Henderson, Lane and Lee were hit—all in that little nullah the arrow is pointing to. Jarrett and I lay at the corner just under where he was killed later on by a sniper firing from the top of the castle turrets. The slope up to Hill 141 was one mass of barbed wire entanglements. The whole beach was enfiladed from where my dugout is now, as you can see, so it is a wonder any escaped alive. They had to dig in. Keep this sketch as it might be useful as a copy for the regimental history . . .'

'*4 June* [to Meta] . . . Lots of fellows are going off their heads out here but personally I've never felt better in my life, I eat and sleep like a pig and feel most awfully cheery . . . Geddes is a ripping commanding officer to work with, but he is frightfully worried and his hair is nearly white. I laugh whenever I see him without his cap, as he had very red hair before. Williams and I don't seem to be affected in the least everyone tells us, but we've both had practically *all* our hair taken off by horse-clippers so it is rather difficult to see if we are becoming prematurely aged! . . .

'I have taken some photos of our dugout. Williams and I have a most awfully comfortable one, but by no means bullet proof as we have had a lot of spent bullets through the roof. "Gallipoli Bill" has just dropped a shell about 20 yards from

where Williams and I are sitting and covered us with earth!
The battalion is in an awful state. It is about 450 short but full
of young soldiers with about 2 months' service. Every now and
then one comes across a familiar face. Nearly all the survivors
of the old lot have been made sgts and corporals. We've lost 5
of our new officers since we've been here. Three of them have
got nerves already after being only five days in the peninsula
and one of them had a bad attack of heart yesterday and has to
go home, so you can imagine how pleasant life is in general. I
don't think it is nearly so exciting as hunting elephants all the
same and very little more dangerous. I am very glad now that I
used to go in for big game shooting as I am sure it is a very good
education for active service! . . .'

'*9 June* [to his mother] . . . The dust is becoming unbearable
here, for there is always a hot wind blowing day and night. We
go up to relieve the firing trenches in 2 or 3 days time but I
don't think there will be any more advancing for some time.
Our losses were appalling the last time we attempted to advance
and the poor old Fusilier Brigade is in a very bad way . . . So
funny that 4 out of the 5 of us left were all together in the hot
weather detachment in Nowshera 4 years ago. This time last
year we were just leaving Mandalay to go up to the Ruby
Mines district! . . . PS I am enclosing a Turkish bullet which
fell between Geddes and me in the dugout last night missing us
both by inches.'

'*13 June*. We have been in the trenches two days now and
have four more to do. The trenches are awful—very badly
made, narrow, not bullet proof and smell absolutely revolting
from dead bodies. We are occupying Turkish trenches which
we captured but there is an absolute maze of trenches. We are
all round the Turks and they are all round us too. The Dublins
have their backs to Achi Baba and face our Base, the Turks
being between them and us! We share several trenches with the
Turks, with a barricade between and throw bombs at each
other over the top!

'The whole place is up and down *hill*, not in the slightest like the trenches in France. To get to our trenches we go four miles up a deep nullah with sides 200 feet high. There is a great barricade right up across the nullah at the furthest point we hold. To get into our trenches we go up a zig-zag track and enter a hole in the cliff which leads into our support trenches and from there are innumerable communication trenches leading into the firing-line. Of course you can't show your head above the trench for a second but have to look through periscopes or through peepholes. Between the trenches are any amount of dead and decomposing bodies of our men and Turks lying on the heather. The smell is awful, though we throw down quantities of Chloride of Lime and creosote . . .

'It is getting on for ten o'clock and has been dark now for over an hour, so there is a tremendous noise going on and one can hardly hear oneself speak. I am in a dugout about a hundred yards from the fire trenches and the Turk bullets are firing into the parapet over my head in great style. It is a most interesting sight to watch. There is no moon at present, so neither side can tell whether an attack is being made. Every few minutes a rocket or flare goes up lighting up the whole scene for a few seconds. Generally there is nothing to see except the heather and about 30 yards away the earth parapet of the enemy's trenches, but sometimes a small party of Turks or our men are shown up, burying dead or sapping under cover of darkness, and a terrific fire is immediately opened up on them. The heather is so thick that a man lying down in it at night is pretty safe to escape being seen, and both the Turks and ourselves send out snipers as soon as it gets dark, to lie between our two lines of trenches.

'I must say I feel very much out of it being back with HQ and it is rotten to feel more or less safe when the men and company officers are in the firing-line, but as Geddes says, we've all had our share at the landing and since and if the five remaining regular officers go now the Battalion will be at an end, for none of these fellows know anything in the way of running a battalion. Sir Ian Hamilton is going round the trenches tomorrow and Geddes and I have to escort the Staff round our lot. It is perfectly awful here now, wherever you dig you come across dead bodies. I got a fatigue party out digging a place for our HQ Mess this morning and we started on four different places before we were able to procure a spot free from dead Turks. The smell is disgusting, but we are all getting used to it now . . .'

'*15 June* . . . The Turks chose last night to attack us at about 8.30 and from then till 3 am I was glued to the 'phone. It was rather critical at one time and we had to send up some men to reinforce the Dublins but it all went off well. There's no doubt the new draft we have out are much too young. In a night show like last night they are very nervous and can hardly be persuaded to fire over the parapets, and any shelling absolutely demoralises them. Luckily we have some very good men left of the original lot who came from India and they hold them together.

'Yesterday afternoon a mail turned up and with it two parcel mails and I have to thank you for a whole crowd of things which are more welcome than I can say. The socks, chocs and watch are all badly wanted and the camera is useful. The book I had read but ages ago and it will be nice to pass the time when we go back to the reserves, the torch most useful last night during the attack as I had to go round hunting up fellows for reliefs and I have been lost since I had to do without one . . .'

'*16 June*. We had a bad night last night—none of us getting a wink of sleep. The Turks share one very important trench with us and we have been sapping out to cut them off. They were evidently getting nervous for at 9 pm last night they suddenly attacked with bombs and hand grenades, so unexpectedly that they turned the Dublins who were holding our part completely out of it and were on a fair way to capturing the whole trench when a fellow of ours in charge of a machine-gun stopped them.

'The Turks came on time after time but only in small numbers and gave no real trouble. We retook a bit of lost trench and killed some 300 Turks, but the thing dragged on right through the night and it wasn't till 8 this morning that the firing ceased. We lost a fellow called Morragh killed and a good man wounded. It was bad luck on Morragh. He came out with the last lot and it was he who stopped the first rush with his machine-gun. He was killed a few minutes afterwards by shrapnel. I have just been up there and the whole place is heaped up with dead and dying Turks and one or two Greeks. They must have been badly caught by the machine-guns. I must go to sleep now and make up for last night, as probably the Turks will again prevent us sapping towards them. No more now.'

The last two of Nightingale's letters to have survived were written over two months later from the northern sector of the peninsula, where the Australians and New Zealanders had been bearing the brunt of the fighting. On 7 August 20,000 fresh troops had been landed at Suvla Bay in an attempt to end the stalemate, but no breakthrough had been achieved by 20 August when the 'incomparable' 29th Division was brought round from Helles to lead a major assault on two dominating hills on the south-east of the Suvla plain—Scimitar Hill and Hill 60. In terms of numbers engaged it was the greatest battle fought in the campaign.

On the afternoon of 21 August, in stifling heat and an unseasonable fog, with a new element of horror in the flames from tinder-dry scrub and gorse set alight by shellfire, the British troops, watched by Sir Ian Hamilton and his staff from a neighbouring height, threw themselves in vain against the Turkish strongholds. There were 5,000 casualties in what Churchill described as 'this dark battlefield of fog and flame'. It was to be the last major action of the campaign.

As Nightingale's letter (dated 25 August) indicates, the British troops were already exhausted when the battle com-

menced, having spent a night being transported by sea from
'V' beach to Suvla, a day under shellfire on the beach and a
night marching to the trenches facing Scimitar Hill.

'. . . Our battalion was the assaulting one of the brigades,
and we had to take a hill about half a mile ahead. Everyone
was cooked with the heat and almost too weary to stand, with
no sleep for 3 nights. At 3 pm the battalion shoved off, 700
strong. The furthest any got was 500 yards and none came
back from there. They all got mown down by machine-gun
fire. We lost 9 officers and nearly 400 men. The Turks shelled
us very heavily and the whole country which is covered with
gorse caught fire. This split up the attack and parties got cut
up. Many of our wounded were burnt alive and it was as nasty
a sight as ever I want to see.

'There were many gallant things done that day. Our doctor
and one of the stretcher bearers went out under a murderous fire
and brought in one officer and 3 men, who were lying out with
broken legs, with the fires creeping up on them. They have
been recommended for the VC, and I hope they get it. Finally
about 7.30 pm the survivors came in under orders from the
division and all night wounded men came straggling back, all
with tales of our men still lying out there.

'How any of us escaped I don't know. Our headquarters was
very heavily shelled and then the fire surrounded the place and
we all thought we were going to be burnt alive. Where the
telephone was, the heat was appalling. The roar of the flames
drowned the noise of the shrapnel, and we had to lie flat at the
bottom of the trench while the flames swept over the top.
Luckily both sides didn't catch simultaneously, or I don't
know what would have happened. After the gorse was all burnt,
the smoke nearly asphyxiated us! All this time our battalion
was being cut up in the open and it really was very unpleasant
trying to send calm messages down to the brigade HQ, while
you were lying at the bottom of the trench like an oven, expecting to be burnt every minute, and knowing that your battalion

was getting hell a hundred yards away! The telephone wires finally fused from the heat.

'The whole attack was a ghastly failure. They generally are now. The Lancs also got rather badly cut up, as they were supposed to follow us in support, but luckily their last company didn't go, nor did the Royal Fusiliers who were after them, for it was sheer suicide and would do no good . . . Geddes and Williams both did awfully good work and escaped being killed dozens of times. We were really played out and so was the whole division and ought never to have been made to do anything. The 29th Division will never be any more good, but the people in authority seem to think we are still the same troops that did the landing.

'That night we were relieved but our brigade was to take over the firing on the left, about 3 miles away. This was our 4th night without sleep and we had a long slow march from 8 pm to 1 am before we reached our new lines. I'd have welcomed a bullet through any part of my anatomy just then and I think most of us would have! Whenever we halted, the men would fall down and sleep and it was an awful job getting them on again. The wonderful thing was that not a man fell out. We finally reached our lines and simply slept in the gorse where we were. The Dublins and the Royals, the two battalions who had taken no part in the attack, took over the firing-line and we were in reserve. We had some men killed in their sleep from bullets coming over the firing-line but nobody cared two straws, we were absolutely done and I would have slept through a bombardment. However at 5.30 am I had to be up again and look for our rations and the battalion was moved at 7 am to a nullah where we now are . . .'

'*26 August* . . . We are now busy making preparations for a winter campaign. No further advance is to be made here by us and all we are going to do is to make some "lines of Torres Vedras" and settle down as comfortably as possible behind them. The country here is very pretty; a combination of

Devonshire and Upper Burma. In places it is exactly like the scrub jungle round Mandalay or Thayetmyo. We are in a little nullah, thick gorse growing all over it, and big grey stones coming up in all directions. There is the dry bed of a stream at the bottom and a few willows to one side. All round the country are patches of wheat and oats, some still growing, some cut, and some standing in sheaves exactly as it was left by the peasants when the landing took place.

'There is no doubt about it, we have played all our cards on this new landing and failed, the opportunity has been lost and if there had been any troops other than only those who took part in it I think they would have done it . . . They shell us all day here, much more so than at Cape Helles, and as I write they are shelling a battery 400 yards immediately behind us and the shells are screaming over my dugout. I am sure everybody's opinion is live and let live, and Turkey for the Turks! . . .'

No further Gallipoli letters from Nightingale have come to light but, supposing he remained with the regiment until the end of the campaign, he would have had other hazards than Turkish shells and bullets to survive. In the blistering heat, tormented by flies, men were reduced to emaciated, dysentery-ridden wrecks. In late November gales swept the peninsula and hundreds drowned in the flooded trenches. Many more died from exposure in the agonising cold that followed. On 2 January Nightingale's battalion was amongst the last to be evacuated from the peninsula, boarding a trawler from the decks of the shell-scarred *River Clyde*, where it had all begun.

The Royal Munster Fusiliers fought on the Western Front from April 1916 until the end of the war, and the regimental history briefly records Nightingale's participation. After the Battle of Cambrai later that year (now with an MC after his name) he took over as second-in-command of his battalion. During the German offensive in the spring of 1918 the battalion was split into two sections and Nightingale was in command of one during actions which 'were examples of indomitable

G

courage, tenacity and stamina and showed that the battalion was well able to carry on the glorious traditions of the "Bengal Europeans" '.

In May 1919 it was Brevet-Major Nightingale who commanded the cadre of his demobilised battalion (thirteen officers and eighty-nine other ranks) when it finally returned to England. Three years later, at the emotional ceremony that marked the dissolution of the Royal Munster Fusiliers, one can imagine that he must have felt that the only part of his life with any meaning had come to an end as King George V spoke of the 'hard fate' that had overtaken a regiment whose 'great deeds are written too clearly in the history of the Empire for anything lightly to efface them', and who undertook to take charge of the regiment's Colours 'to be preserved and held in reverence at Windsor Castle as a perpetual record of your noble exploits in the field'.

The last mention of Nightingale in the Army List is of his posting to the Lincolnshire Regiment with the rank of captain in January 1923. That eight years of mostly active service found him on the same rung of the Army ladder is surprising and might well suggest some character defect not apparent in the letters. Of what transpired in the post-war years, a road to despair, only one person could tell, his sister Meta, but her memories are locked within her. The only clues are to be found among the possessions that have passed from her to her daughter and from Mrs Coleman's hearsay recollections.

From a bureau at her home in Crystal Palace, London, Mrs Coleman brings to light photograph albums, scattered snapshots, regimental souvenirs, a family tree. It is an elaborate and imposing family tree, branching back to a Nitingall of 1473 and the fact that its research was instigated by Nightingale himself might suggest the quest of a man seeking the assurance of family roots, a sense of belonging.

Mrs Coleman recalls having heard that her uncle was at one time engaged to a Swedish girl, but that nothing came of it.

She does not know when, or why, he left the army. All she gleaned about his life thereafter was that he was a keen sportsman and went on salmon fishing trips to Ireland, that he took to drinking heavily, lived on his own in a cottage in the Somerset village of Wedmore near the Cheddar Gorge, and that it was there, on 18 April 1935, that he shot himself.

The 'charmed life' that had survived Gallipoli only to be thrown away as insupportable twenty years later haunts one as the faded snapshots give glimpses of Nightingale as he was at moments in the past. In tropical gear and white pith-helmet, neat-moustached, standing proudly beside 'my first elephant shot in Burma, 1912': in a Gallipoli dug-out, with crew-cut hair and a confident gaze: smart in officer's uniform somewhere on the Russian-Polish frontier in 1921. But it is in two very dissimilar pictures—of Guy as a small boy and of his mother in old age—that the key may be found to the tragedy of a life that, at the time of the Gallipoli letters, seemed so full of youthful ardour and endeavour.

A pastel portrait of the widowed Mrs Nightingale reveals a face of time-ravaged beauty, the face it might be of some Dame of the theatre, haughty, accustomed to respect. 'She was not well off in later life, lived on her own but could cope in any circumstance,' says Mrs Coleman. And then, looking at the portrait, she recalls that her grandmother, on her deathbed, had spoken briefly to her about her son and had said: 'Of course the trouble with Guy was that he was always weak.'

The studio photograph of the young Guy is in an ornate, mother-of-pearl frame, hinged to a similarly framed photograph of his ringleted sister Meta. One can imagine it standing in a place of honour in the parents' living-room in Delhi, commented on by solicitous guests wondering how the dear children were getting on in far-away England. It is a picture, knowing the circumstances, that touches the heart: of a small boy in a sailor suit, unsmiling, lost-looking and forlorn.

5   *Engineer on Horseback*

When Robert Charles Case enlisted as a trooper in the Royal Wiltshire Yeomanry in September 1914, there were doubts in few minds that the war would soon be over and that a decisive role would be played, as in past wars, by our mounted troops.

A farmer's son aged twenty-one, Case was nearing the completion of five years' training at the Great Western Railway Works at Swindon, had recently been awarded the Chairman's prize for the highest marks gained in the Technical School, and was a good deal more skilled as an engineer than a horseman. But, together with a number of fellow-trainees, he had little hesitation in opting for the saddle. 'The feeling was that it was going to be a jolly good sporting show,' he recalls today, 'and that we'd see some fun with a Yeomanry regiment.'

In many peoples' memories at the outbreak of the war were the achievements of the British cavalry during the Boer War, and, despite the new age of the automobile and aeroplane that had since dawned, few could envisage a war in which the horse was not of prime importance. Such an assumption seemed confirmed at the outset with chilling reports of the Uhlans (German cavalry) in action during the retreat from Mons, spearheading the advance as the tanks of the Panzer Divisions were to do in World War II.

Case's early letters home give a bizarre glimpse of the

rigorous equestrian training going on in many parts of the country while the armies in France slowly sank into the mud. From hindsight there is an air of the ludicrous in his descriptions of cross-country manoeuvres, of mounted troops against armoured cars and motorcyclists, of a civilian airing his dog on the Sussex Downs running for his life as a squadron of khaki-clad horsemen thunder suddenly towards him. A photograph Case sent to his parents, depicting himself in full battle array on his 'war-horse', with an accompanying list of the numerous items that weighed them down, brings irresistibly to mind the encumbered White Knight in *Alice through the Looking Glass*.

It was not until it had become transparently clear that an ability to jump Grand National-type obstacles, to urge a horse over the edge of a quarry or into the swirling eddies of a river, had little bearing on the confrontation of an enemy over the barbed wire of no man's land, that Case began to pull strings for a transfer to the Royal Engineers. An added incentive had been the advent of a Regular Army adjutant whose parade ground bark was deeply resented by the troopers. Most of the officers were territorials like themselves, county gentry whose horsemanship had been acquired on the hunting field, the point-to-point course and the polo ground, and the troopers had readily accepted their idiosyncrasies. To be required to knuckle down to the theirs-not-to-reason-why subservience of the regular seemed like an insult.

It was in 1972 that Case donated to the Imperial War Museum two bound volumes containing typescript copies of the scores of letters he wrote home during four and a half years of active service that took him from the Western Front to Macedonia, Egypt and Palestine, liberally illustrated with contemporary photographs and documents. Early on he had suggested his parents might keep his letters as 'possibly affording interesting reading in the years to come, for we shall never get a time like this again—at least let us hope not'.

The letters, for all their high spirits and humour, reveal a mounting disillusionment with the war he had embarked on with such enthusiasm. Writing from the Western Front in 1916 he is recoiling at the spectacle of 'the most cultivated nations upon earth (as we smugly imagine ourselves) waging the dirtiest and most unsporting warfare that could possibly be imagined'. By the end of the war, now a company commander with two mentions in despatches for 'gallant and distinguished services in the field', he has come to a realisation of 'how terrible and how horribly futile all this suffering seems to be'.

Final disillusionment came on his return from the Middle East to the promised 'land fit for heroes' to find the GWR offering him thirty shillings a week to complete the six months of training he had forgone by volunteering. In disgust he 'shook the dust of England from off my feet' for a career in India, where he eventually reached the top as an administrator with the India State Railways. Today, at the home of his widowed sister in Sidmouth, Devon, where he has lived since the death of his wife, he still talks bitterly of the aftermath of the war. 'The government battened upon the courage and loyalty of innumerable young men, fought the war cheaply and largely at their expense, and abandoned them to their fate when they were no longer needed.'

What kept Case going through the war, as evidenced by his letters, was a level-headed approach to any new experience, comradeship and a sense of humour. And in the two sections of letters that follow—covering his Yeomanry training and his six months on the Western Front with the Royal Engineers— one can sense a maturing process as he becomes more deeply involved, less glib with his judgements. Ridicule of the type of Regular Army officer who 'foams at the mouth and shrieks with rage simply because some poor inoffensive little devil happens to turn to the right instead of to the left' develops into a boundless admiration for the Tommy in the trenches— 'Never despise the Infantryman for he is the most uncomplaining sufferer in this wretched war.' Whatever his feelings about the purpose and the prosecution of the war, it is evident that he learned much about human nature. It is not surprising to learn that among his surviving friends today he still counts the sergeant-major who had served under him in France and until the end of the war in the Middle East.

Case's boyhood home was his father's 360 acre mixed farm near Bridgewater in Somerset. Horses were part and parcel of daily life. In addition to fourteen cart horses there were two hunters, on which his father and elder brother rode regularly to hounds. One of his earlier memories is of riding his Exmoor pony to the village school, from which at the age of nine he gained a scholarship to a public school.

Case as a boy was not keen on riding. 'I was more of a book-worm—Hans Anderson, Sir Walter Scott, Henty, Ballantyne, all the adventure stuff.' During his apprenticeship years, by which time the family had moved to another farm in Gloucester-shire, he took to occasional foxhunting and became a crack shot on deer culling stalks with an uncle. But his most prized possession was a 'Scott' motorcycle. A photograph taken during his first leave shows him as proudly astride it, in trooper's uniform, as on the saddle of his 'war-horse', his mother en-sconced in the basketwork sidecar, spaniel on lap.

In 1914 the horse still dominated the English scene and thousands were taken over by the Army, together with ship-ments from abroad, particularly the Argentine. From thorough-bred to van-horse, they were as mixed a collection as the officers and men who made up the Yeomanry. Case recalls that many who joined with him—railway trainees, local teachers, clerks, shop assistants—had never ridden a horse and pays retrospective tribute to the speed with which they were inured to the saddle.

In a letter accompanying a group photograph of the Regi-ment's officers, in April 1915, Case's summary sets the tone of gentlemanly amateurism:

'Colonel Thynne, a dour, stern man, and unrivalled fault finder: Captain and late Adjutant Noel Edwards, fine fellow, of polo fame: Captain Lakin, present Adjutant, just back from the front: L. Lockyre-Lampson, a very fine type of the real gentleman, MP for Salisbury, 80% failure as a soldier: Major Palmer, the one and only, finest rider to hounds in the Beaufort Hunt: Major Fuller, M.F.H. Cricklade Hunt: Lt. Somerville, an awful egg, but quite a decent fellow: Lord Alec Thynne, a good old sport, despite his martial glare.'

Although the Royal Wiltshire Yeomanry was Britain's oldest Yeomanry regiment (founded in 1797, disbanded in 1967 when the Territorial Army was abolished) Case recalls no harping on tradition. Until the appointment of Major Palmer as adjutant, the officers' barks were generally worse than their bites and there was an overall feeling of improvisation in the training. No one was even quite sure what the function of the Yeomanry would be in a semi-mechanised war, though it was accepted that death-and-glory cavalry charges would be the province of the professional Guards' regiments (a few such did occur when fighting on the Western Front broke into the open). In effect the Yeomanry were trained as mounted infantrymen, mobile enough to take the enemy by surprise by galloping to an attacking position before dismounting and opening fire. Practice in rifle shooting and bayonet fighting were at least an asset by the time it had been decided to dismount most of the Yeomanry regiments and convert them into infantry.

During his eleven months' training as a trooper before obtaining a commission in the Royal Engineers, Case was stationed at a camp near East Grinstead in Sussex, 'in most beautiful country very high up and commanding a huge expanse of heavily wooded undulating downs'. Most of the initial complaints—the drudgery of drill, fatigues, guard duties, the primitive overcrowded huts, the mud, rain and cold—have been omitted from the extracts that follow. Emphasis has been given to Case's reactions to a ludicrously outdated training that was still going strong long after the war had become a subterranean struggle for survival under the scream of shells.

Many of Case's letters were written to be passed around the family, and begin 'Dear People'. Individual recipients are here indicated only when pertinent. His first lengthy description of a manoeuvre is given in full as indicating with what purposefulness he embarked on the training, though already with a sense of the unreality of it all.

'*2 November 1914* . . . We had quite an exciting day last week when we were the 'defenders' and the other squadrons had to practise reconnaissance and try to get through our lines. Our section was sent out about 3 miles as a picket, and we had hardly reached our position when we spotted a troop (30 men) of the enemy branching down a side road, just in front of us. I was sent back at once to our signalling station and gave a message to warn our main body. We must refer to the sketch map to make things plain. I was just going to leave (H) when I heard firing at (K) and, on going down to investigate, found the enemy had overpowered our picket at (E) and were overpowering our resistance at (K).

'I saw at once that our men on the JIE road must either be warned or get a very hot time of it, as they were surrounded and cut off, while they were probably not aware of it. It was of course highly improbable that they would be there by the time I came back again, but it was a good excuse and I wanted to try my own unaided efforts at scouting and cross-country work. So off I went in a westerly direction, as I hoped to locate the troop who had gone down the (J) road, and also to outflank their patrols.

'It turned out that I had bitten off just about as much as I could chew, for the enemy seemed to be swarming everywhere. I dared not go on the road at all for obvious reasons, and even thus I met the enemy snake-patrols 4 times. They bolted twice and I bolted twice. I was only fired at once, and then I should have got in first only my rifle jammed owing to the badly fitting blanks in the magazine. After this I carried the rifle at full cock with a blank in the breach; luckily for me, as it turned out.

'It was the first time I had the opportunity of trying my *own* nag across the country, and the first jump was over some rails about 4 feet high. He went at it gamely enough, but more or less fell over; still, he is only 4 years old and will no doubt improve with practice. Anyhow the rails secured me from further pursuit on the part of certainly 90 per cent of the enemy, so it was well worth the trouble.

'We now come to where I at last reached my objective, Saint Hill (I). There was a bend in the ride through the wood where I was, which was only about 10 yards from the road. On rounding this judge of my surprise when I saw on the opposite side of the road 2 of the enemy picket sitting in the hedge, their mouths full of bread and cheese, and their horses' nosebags on. They did not hear me until I was practically upon them and shouted "Hands up". They were fairly staggered, and after getting over the shock ran for their rifles and covered me. I didn't shoot, as being close, the wads (rifle blanks) might have proved dangerous, so there we stood, or rather THEY stood, for I was still on my nag! The situation struck me as being so ridiculous that I burst out laughing, and then they too saw the joke.

'In the arbitration that followed I suggested that the best way out of the difficulty was to cry quits, and they were quite satisfied. To finish off the jest, I dismounted and put on my horse's nosebag, had some lunch myself and a yarn with them. My nag had got about half way through his feed when I heard the most tremendous clattering of horses galloping down the road. I thought "This is no place for me!" and without stopping even to take off the nosebag, or put in the bit, hopped on my nag and fairly tore off back into the wood. Finding a place where I could conceal myself I stopped, adjusted things a bit and picked my way back to (B).

'It was very amusing to hear the surprised queries of "Hello then, did you escape?", for everyone thought that capture must have been my fate, as I had been away so long. I was able to report to my officer the position of the enemy whom I had spotted between (I) and (K), feeding their horses, as I came back. It was a most interesting day, and after a bit I shall try to "work" things so that I can get another such . . .

'We had a field day last week when the whole Regiment and the Royal Hants Artillery turned out to fight about 100 motor (armoured) cars, plus maxims on sidecars, plus scores of motor-cycles. It was a very dull day for our troop, we had to furnish a guard for the Artillery, so we couldn't see or do a thing except watch the RHA fire off 8 rounds. We therefore stuck in a beastly field, wet through and shivering, all day long. Our antagonists were Royal Navy men, and they apparently wiped the floor with us, for they got our fellows out into the open by showing themselves and pretending to attack, and when our men had dismounted turned on dozens of machine-guns. There was hardly a man left to tell the tale, or there wouldn't have been had the affair been a serious one instead of a sham fight. Still, it will be a very wholesome lesson to our officers, and I'll bet they will not be caught napping a second time . . .'

'*6 November* . . . We have now entered upon a new phase in our existence in as much that we are now what we call "barrack room" soldiers; our main object in life being apparently to shine and keep shining. There are in the neighbourhood of, I should say, 500 buttons (one can hardly count them accurately as they dazzle one's eyes so), saddlery, boots, rifles etc etc to clean and shine, and shine again the next day just the same, for the things tarnish and grow dull during the night. We are now in the habit of using our bandoliers as shaving mirrors, and on inspection the officers have to wear coloured spectacles to protect them from the glare.

'Sundays are now days of toil and grave anxiety, for we get about one hour in which to clean and shine, wash and shave, and so on, and then, while still sweating with rage and in anything but a religious frame of mind, we are lined up on church parade, after having been carefully examined by the lieut, and then even more carefully by the squadron cdr, who carries a microscope and a dust-detector. The regiment is then called to "Shun", while the colonel and major, who is the second-in-command, followed by the adjutant, lieutenant, regimental sgt-major, orderly sgt, "and others", walk slowly, and very slowly too, down the front and up the rear of each rank. Should any luckless wretch be found with any foreign matter upon his clothes or accoutrements, he is haled forth and usually sentenced to be shot at dawn. Yes, it's a hard, grim life.

'After church there is usually a kit inspection, which it would appear is a favourite pastime amongst our officers, as they order kit inspections on every possible occasion. This time I caused much amusement by draping my identity disc around the neck of my old clay pipe, that awful "Brazenose" thing I showed you when we were down at Chippenham. The best of it was the major did not happen to spot the disc and asked me for it. I said, as cool as cucumber, "There it is, sir." He passed on quick!'

'*14 November*. Dear Dad, You will doubtless be pleased to learn that my nag is nearly as high as your old hunter, although of a good deal slighter build. He was bred by a thoroughbred from a van-horse, but I am afraid he has not the lustrous eye and spreading nostril which goes with the blood horse. We do our drill upon a sort of heath which reminds me very much of some parts of the Quantocks. It seems to be a particularly unsuitable place for horses, as the heather covers over the most treacherous holes, which have been dug all over the place for some unknown reason. In several localities there are soft bogs, into which a horse will instantly sink up to his belly, and today we rode into one with the result that 2 fellows were pitched off over their horses' heads. Usually our drill consists of sending out a few scouts to reconnoitre a position, and then when they have reported "no enemy" we make a "bound" across the valley and secure that position. This process is repeated till we have reached the desired position . . .'

'*19 December.* Today I took part in my first regimental drill. This means that every available man turns out and the colonel takes command. We were about 350 strong and as a preliminary got thoroughly wet and chilled to the bone by an icy rain which was seconded in its efforts by an equally cold and strong wind. The wetting process was finished off during the drill by sundry storms, judiciously timed, so that when our spirits and personal warmth rose to one degree above zero, they were speedily lowered again.

'Anyhow, the drill teemed with so many interesting incidents and it was so vastly amusing to see first the colonel chew up his majors, and then the majors curse the troop-leaders, and they in their turn the men, that my own discomfort was drawn away by these scenes, in the same way as an exterior application will ease a toothache. The drill came to an end at last, but I am afraid it was not a brilliant success, for the ground was fairly honeycombed with rabbit holes, and the fellows were mostly too concerned in dodging them to pay much attention to orders. Altogether, I am afraid our fellows on the whole are not what one could call DASHING riders! . . .

'I gave the Colonel an unasked-for exhibition of trick-riding the other day when he requested us, in his usual engaging manner, to mount on the NEAR side, instead of the off, as we usually do. My nag is very high (or tall, I don't know which is the correct term) and very restive, and after getting my foot in the stirrup I was on the point of slinging over my rifle, when the brute made a rearward movement. I instantly decided to hop up as far as the saddle and throw over the rifle while still standing in the one stirrup. Alas for my plans! The nag immediately swirled into the ranks, breaking them up and scattering them like leaves before the autumn wind, while I had to leave go the rifle and devote all my time to the steering gear, at the same time trying frantically to cock my other leg over the saddle.

'The leg being coaxed half way over was of course arrested in

113

its flight by the bally rifle, and eventually I reluctantly decided to abandon the idea. All this time, mind you, I was gyrating and sidestepping, or rather the nag was, like a frisky waltzer. Anyhow, as I have said, I reluctantly abandoned the idea and dismounted, muttering softly to myself, and after readjusting myself and accoutrements remounted without further incident. The colonel was so struck and astonished with my performance that he omitted to censure me for not promptly obeying his order!

'My other noteworthy feat of horsemanship was to mount and dismount on the other side, without touching the saddle, in record time. We had been standing, horse holding, for about 2 hours, and were nearly frozen solid, and I was so delighted to get the chance of getting warm again that on the order to mount, I gave such an enormous spring that I flew right over the saddle, and alighted on my hands the other side. The movement was done with such agility and grace that only 2 fellows noticed it, which, as you may imagine, caused me much vexation . . .'

'*27 December* . . . The last few days have been simply a mad orgy for most of us, and the piles of empty beer and whisky bottles which have accumulated are a sight worth seeing. Hours spent in putting various fellows, in various stages of intoxication, to bed and restraining their ardour to get up, either to dance or to fight . . .'

'*3 January* . . . Here's some gossip, all more or less official and not more than 3rd hand. The discipline at the front is rigid. Several cases of self-mutilation have occurred in order to escape from the firing line to the doubtful mercies of hospital. The extreme penalty is now being paid for all cases where the crime is brought home. If the bolt of a rifle is lost the offender gets 28 days CB and spends from 2 to 4 hours each day tied to a cart wheel. Pretty hot, isn't it . . .'

'*22 January.* Enclosed pleased find 2 photos which should go as a pair, of myself and "the war-horse". I had a view of both sides taken so that the whole of the outfit can be seen. Equipped thus we are in "full marching order" and ready for "trekking" any distance in reason, to sleep out and so on. I will give a list of the articles and it may afford you some amusement to try to pick them out in the photos.

'(1) my noble self (2) gallant steed (3) saddle (4) bridle (5) horse blanket (6) bed blanket (7) waterproof ground sheet (8) 3 cloak straps (9) 2 horseshoes in shoe case (10) 2 pegs with shackle (11) built-up rope (12) nosebag containing 2 pecks of oats (13) mess tin (14) rifle in bucket (15) head stall and rope. On myself is carried (1) regulation uniform (2) bandoliers (3) waist-belt (4) bayonet (5) water bottle (6) haversack containing 1 housewife, toilet articles, towels and rations and a holdall. Besides all this there are the transport waggons, on which are carried 1 kitbag per man, in which is 1 pair of boots, 1 pair of socks, 2 flannel shirts and 1 pair pants; besides which, in cold weather, 1 blanket per man is carried . . .

'We were taken to our "Grand National" Jumping School, and I can tell you the excitement was intense. The EXTREME edge of excitement was taken off when we were told only to jump the trench and rail jumps. Mirabile dictu, every horse in the squadron was either coaxed or beaten over, and not a single rider was emptied from his saddle. After this came the event of the day! Those horses which appeared to be able to jump were noted and their riders were given the option of having a go at the "Grand National Jump", a jump with rails and furze, the top rail of which comes just level with my head. Amidst a fair bubbling of excitement "yours truly" with about 15 aspirants for death or glory, stalked forth and avowed our fixed intention of "going over". I got over capitally alongside my troop officer, as did the majority, but the last 5 or 8 men played the deuce, for they more or less fell through the gaps that the first lot of horses had made, and they fairly tore the jump to pieces . . .'

'*31 January* [from a long description of another field day, in which the "enemy" were the Hants Carabineers, defending an

ammunition column at Edenbridge] . . . I happened to go out
as 2nd man in the snake-patrol (a very creepy job as it was
foggy) and just outside Hartfield we ran into two of the enemy.
We nipped off our horses and had 2 shots at them in less than
no time. They scooted off and after getting reinforced we
followed them and drove them down a valley and eventually
cut them off, after they had been obviously "shot" dozens of
times. These 2 were an officer and orderly of the Hants.

'They at last decided to be made prisoners and the non-com
in charge of the section took the officer's horse and the skunk
actually spurred his horse violently and tried to break away
again. This, mind you, after having been manifestly shot
several times! The non-com remonstrated with the skunk and
asked him to play the game. The skunk then lugged out a huge
·45 revolver and pointed it at the non-com. Well, I always had
the idea that I was so phlegmatical that I could not lose my
temper. I was mistaken. At this I must admit I fairly lost my
wool and called the officer a dirty skunk and things rather worse
and threatened to knock him over the head with my rifle if he
couldn't "play the game". He got somewhat ruffled at this, and
told me that I was speaking to an officer. I said, in anything
but an apologetic tone of voice, "I beg your pardon, Sir, but we
usually PLAY THE GAME IN THE *ROYAL WILTS!*" This
last shot went right home, and he was led off to our HQ.
Shortly after this I was shot dead, no doubt as a punishment for
my language! . . .

'*28 February* . . . We have for the last few days been busy dis-
infecting horses, and all things appertaining thereto. The
blankets have been baked, and rugs also baked, the horses
washed, the saddles stripped and dipped in Condy's grooming
kit soaked in disinfectant and so on. Very grave "official"
orders have been given out as regards hygiene, such as "at
least 2 windows on the leeward side of each hut must be kept
open all night. If the rain blows in arrangements must be made
accordingly." "All blankets must be shaken once a day."

"Personal cleanliness is most essential and easy access to baths should be afforded for the troops." "The huts should be kept scrupulously clean." All very fine, but rather sardonic, I fancy! . . .'

'*23 March*. We had a rotten "suck in" on Friday. On Thursday a telegram arrived, the immediate consequence of which was to cancel all leave and to recall all those already on leave, and to make us all simmer with excitement. We were awakened at about 5 am by a motorbike tearing up to the camp and the rider running round to the Orderly Room. In about 10 minutes we were all turned out into the cold and told to get into full marching order. We had ammunition, hay, meat, blankets and 101 other things all loaded up in less than no time; breakfast was served out at 6.45 and we moved out of camp at 7.15. About 5 miles out we joined the rest of the Brigade and were told that the German Fleet were out and had landed a party at Brighton, while 2 Zeppelins were over London during the night. We had to take up an advanced line of outposts south west of Lewes. Ten minutes afterwards we learned that it was all a scare, and the "binding was considerable" . . .

'My confounded nag has actually developed acute ringworm! The awful brute is too chronic for words. He went dead lame on a 30 mile trek and he goes lame on every possible occasion, slithers and slides about these tarred roads like a smooth-treaded tyre, and fairly goes out of his way to prove himself an absolute and complete dud . . .'

'*24 April* . . . The hottest thing we have done so far is to ride down over the edge of a quarry, and a deuced nasty place it is too. One fellow rolled clean over his horse's head, through not leaning back over his saddle far enough. I am making a rough sketch of the place from which you will see that it was a sheer drop over the edge that looked so desperate I should never have thought horses would have gone over. Strange to say, the only accident that has occurred so far during our training happened today when one man, who was out by himself on a combat patrol, fell off and somehow broke his leg and ankle and dislocated his thigh . . .'

'*15 May*. I never remember being so really delighted and relieved in my life as when yesterday I found my dear old gee had returned from the isolation lines. After the horrible seat-pulverising that I had to put up with riding other nags during the last couple of months I will forgive the dear old "Hun" his little ways of slipping and tripping and rearing etc. I really think he knew me again, for when I went over to talk to and caress him, and after smelling me over for a few moments, he whinnied and licked my grimy paw . . . He is now picketed out by himself in the open for a week or fortnight's further quarantine. Of course he's a pretty miserable looking object after his sickness and his hair is all spotted like a leopard where the ringworms have been burnt out . . .'

'*4 June* . . . There was a very distressing accident which occurred just outside our place on Thursday last. A young fellow of the RAMC fell somehow out of a gig and got his foot caught in the strap which fastens the breeching to the shaft. The horse, of course, bolted and the wretched fellow was dragged a quarter of a mile with his head and body dragging on the road and being terribly buffeted by the horse's hoofs and the spokes on the wheels.

'We ran out and stopped the horse and cut the poor fellow down. He was a terrible sight! There was a deep wound in the side of his head, caused probably by a kick, one of his eyes was punctured, his arm was broken, his shoulder dislocated and his ribs staved in. Besides all these awful injuries he was very badly hurt with the dragging along the road, his head and back being worn away to the bone. The unfortunate fellow was immediately seen to by the RAMC but he never recovered consciousness and died late in the afternoon . . .'

'*5 July*. Up on the hills there is a most magnificent space of rolling down covered with springy turf, available for drill, and I would like you to have seen us the other day when we formed squadron-line and cantered and then galloped as hard as we could lick for half a mile. The thudding of the hoofs was like thunder. A very comic touch was put to the scene by a civilian and a dog who were about 500 yards ahead of us when the "Gallop" was given. He looked at us for about 2 seconds, fairly petrified with astonishment, and then suddenly took to his heels and ran for his life. We should have roared with laughter if we hadn't been so busy looking after our horses and keeping our alignment!

'The horse swimming has great possibilities for fun, but owing to our spoil-sport of a major who treats everything as a parade, there isn't much joy about it, but instead devilish hard work. The river, a tidal one with a 4 mile per hour current, is about 50 yards wide and an endless rope is put across and manned. The horses are brought up and tied on the rope at reasonable intervals, six at a time. The men then pull the six over the river and others untie them and so on till every horse has got over. About 20 horses are got over first of all with men swimming with them. This is the only sporting part about the job. The saddles and kits are towed across on rafts. My job is to sit in a boat with another fellow as oarsmen and stand by to "save life" . . .'

'*14 July* . . . We were very angry one day for we were even more fooled than ever. All our clothes were wet from the previous day's rain, but we were ripped out of bed at 2.30 am by the "Alarm" and told to get into full marching order and abandon our lines to the Sussex Yeomanry who were taking our places, and so on, and so forth, with a lot more damnable lies. Well, we trekked out about 2 miles out, and then halted; after some delay an officer came round wanting to know what we had in our holsters. After more delay we were calmly informed that the whole thing was a "put up" job! As I told our officer afterwards it is *absolutely criminal* to fool and tamper with the men's keenness and enthusiasm in this uncalled-for manner. I think he appreciated the way we looked at it. Anyway, we didn't get anything to eat or drink till 9.30 am and after that we had horse swimming, drill and inspections with not the slightest allowance for our extra work.

'With regard to the above-mentioned fooling, none of us would object overmuch to these alarms, although they are certainly a confounded nuisance, if they didn't tell us so many lies over the job. We should turn out just as quickly or quicker if they didn't try to lead us to believe that "the day" has at last arrived. After all, we are not a blithering pack of fools! This is an instance of the lack of imagination of a Regular Commander, who all his life has commanded Regular Army men, and who now cannot see the difference in the mode of treatment desirable with a totally different style of man that he has under him in the Territorials, and Yeomanry at that . . .'

Case gave vent to this outburst, specifically aimed at the martinet Major Palmer, the day before he learned that he had obtained a commission in the 3/3rd London Field Company, Royal Engineers. The eleven months of training that followed were closely geared to actual conditions on the Western Front, and Case's letters during this period, from training camps in Essex, Hertfordshire and Wiltshire, are largely concerned with the art of digging trenches, dugouts, field fortifications and mines, building bridges and rafts of various kinds, and the use of high explosives. But that a degree of horsemanship was required even of Royal Engineer officers is indicated in his first letter: 'Fortunately I can ride, so have been let off the riding school. The poor devils of subalterns undergoing this painful course are mostly pretty raw and painfully stiff.'

Case's reaction to achieving officer status is tersely stated, with Major Palmer no doubt still in mind: 'I fear I shall never manage to develop the real army curtness, to call it by a polite name; for one thing, I can't be sufficiently unmannerly without inflicting considerable personal loss of self-respect on myself, and for another, I can't help looking at the humorous side of things. It strikes me as being supremely ridiculous to see a man fairly foam at the mouth and shriek with rage, simply because some poor inoffensive little devil happens to turn to the right instead of to the left, or something equally futile. It really seems so completely out of proportion.'

Two other letters from this period may be quoted from as indicating how remote from the reality of the trenches was the soldier still in training, how he grasped at any clue as to what it would be like.

In Case's description of a full-scale Field Day, without the charade of mounted troops, there is a premonition of no man's land. '. . . About 3 pm a general action started and from my position ¾ mile from the firing-line I obtained an excellent view of the proceedings through the binoculars which Uncle Harry gave me. These infantry attacks seem very slow after being used to the rattling actions of mounted infantry. All the same, it is really very uncanny to watch a huge line of men, looking like so many ants, and gradually, yet surely, getting nearer and nearer their objective. Their advance seems to be quite irresistible in spite of all the machine-guns in the world . . .'

In his retelling of some 'astounding yarns from fellows recently back from Flanders', one can sense a stiffening of the sinews behind the laughter of those still to be initiated into a world where violence had become a virtue. 'These yarns all point to the fact that the mind gets quite used to the whole affair after a few days and jokes are made of things that wouldn't seem the least funny in ordinary civil life. About the funniest of the whole lot, and one that made us fairly rock with laughter, largely because of the way it was told, comes from Garrard.

' "During a very hasty retreat by the English, a burly German was seen who had been cut off from his own crowd, running back with our men, hoping to escape in the confusion. A sapper spotted him, let out a yell of surprise and annoyance, fairly leapt after him, the German bolting like a frightened hare, and after a ding-dong race of 50 yards or so overhauled him and, with a mighty effort, sliced off the Hun's pate with a single blow of his shovel."

'Another charming incident: "In a certain trench about 4 miles south of Ypres, a French soldier lies buried in the side of the trench with one hand sticking out from the side. It is considered that, unless this hand is shaken and the owner of the hand wished 'Good Luck' on going up to these particular trenches, bad luck will attend the neglectors of this ceremony." Just one more: "Before any decent-sized attack, orders are issued to the effect that if any prisoners are taken they will be fed from our own men's rations." '

Case's last letter before going to the Front records four days' leave in Somerset, back in the tranquil country scenes of his boyhood, rifle in hand but aimed at no human quarry. Ironically it is the only mention in his letters of a shot fired by him to kill.

'*3 June* . . . The country is looking too beautiful for description, and there are splendid crops of hay and corn. On Thursday night and Friday morning I went out with Uncle's Mauser to shoot a couple of black deer which were harbouring in Heer Wood, or "Hurod" as they call it down here. We fairly ransacked the whole locality but, although we could see the fresh spoor, there was absolutely no trace of them to be found. However, I had the pleasure of seeing a beautiful red deer about 500 yards off and watched him grazing for some time, as I didn't want to shoot a beast like that. He eventually loped off to his harbour in the thickets of Smokeham.

'This morning, Saturday, I rose at dawn, after jossing down on Ned Flatman's, the gamekeeper's, sofa, and hied me to Broadwood. There I spotted a three-quarters-grown deer grazing outside the wood, and after a short stalk I let him have it in the right place at about 80 yards range. He trotted off, apparently quite unconcerned, but we noticed a big hole in his ribs. After going about 25 yards, he suddenly dropped like a log. Extraordinary thing wasn't it? We found afterwards that the whole top of the heart and a large part of the lungs had been blown clean away.'

Case arrived in France shortly before the infantry went over the top, on 1 July 1916, to launch the Battle of the Somme, the doomed Allied offensive in which the British were to lose 420,000 casualties, the French 200,000 and the Germans 450,000 by the time it ended in the same stalemate four months later. For much of this period Case was on a relatively quiet sector of the Front some twenty miles from the Somme north of Arras, but though not directly engaged in the battle he was constantly aware of it. 'We can see the dull red flash of the explosions, see the sky lit up with star shells and on still nights feel the ground quivering even here. One fails to conceive how flesh and blood can stand the strain.'

Case was not to experience the ultimate horrors of trench warfare, but his letters are notable in giving a very clear picture of what it felt like for a newcomer to find himself at the front line for the first time. For him the reality was overwhelmingly different from what he had imagined during nearly two years of anticipatory preparation. Those early mock battles on horseback over the English countryside must have seemed more than ever laughable as he took his first look across no man's land at the 'miles of trenches, populated by scores of thousands of men, and yet one cannot see a living soul'. It was the anonymity of it all, the casualness of death as the guns on both sides sent over their daily quota of shells, that finally dispelled any conception of war as 'sporting'.

Case's company occupied trenches near Vimy Ridge in a sector noted for the labarynthine windings of its trenches, field fortifications and mine workings, and the engineers were kept busy. The scarcity value of skilled RE officers and sappers at this time is indicated in one letter: 'Our lives are conserved to an embarrassing extent, all officers and men being withdrawn from the line back to billets as soon as there is news of an impending attack.' It was the Yeomanry officer who had proved expendable. His old regiment was one of the few still spared the indignity of being dismounted (that came in 1918). But, as recorded in the official history of the Royal Wiltshire Yeomanry, its main duties in France were menial ones: 'traffic control, escort for POW's, working parties, manning of observation posts and other duties for which they were not primarily trained'.

The 60th Division, to which the 3/3rd Field Company, Royal Engineers, belonged, landed in France on 21 June 1916. Case's impressions on the journey to the front are given in a letter to his sister on 25 June: 'Some of the things that struck me most are as follows: the almost absolute impossibility of realising that there is a war in progress, even now although we are in sound of the guns 20 miles away, even though we can see the lights from the star shells and in some cases the flashes of the explosions. The little village we are in is as quiet as any little West Country town. The fact that during the whole train journey I suppose we did not notice more than 6 civilians. The quiet, and one might call it sneaking way in which we moved off to our present destination—not a cheer, hardly any conversation above an occasional order, not a martial sound of any description, not even a glance from passers-by. I suppose the sight of troops is much too common for anyone to take any notice nowadays. There seems to be a quiet and confident look about everything that goes on and it is quite impossible to realise that we are "in the soup" at last . . .'

'*3 July* . . . The Company split up and I took my section up to the support lines, where we were all stuck into dugouts like so many rabbits. Personally I was taken over by a jolly fine fellow in the Royal Scots Pioneers. Nearly all the old hands here are Scotch, and I find the men magnificent workers, and as fine fellows in their way as the officers.

'Our work is on deep dugouts, with 20 feet of head cover, and very heavy timbering. We draw up to 75 infantry per 24 hours to help us in the work. The poor old infantry get a pretty thin time out here as they are "the hewers of wood and carriers of water" for themselves and everyone else. It cannot be a very humorous proceeding to have to carry timbers 9" × 7' 0" along hundreds of yards of trenches, wriggling round corners like worms, slipping up on greasy duckboards etc.

'It is a very weird sensation to be under fire for the first time. Up to the present we have only experienced shell fire, for one rarely hears the bark of a rifle, and only occasionally a machine-gun. The shells and trench mortars, grenades and so on, how-ever, are practically continuous during the periods of strafe. These periods are quite distinct and last in a very concentrated mixture from ½ hour to 2 hours. The amazing part of it is that no one appears to get damaged and, except that the trenches are blown to little bits, no good or evil appears to be done. During the night the whole skyline is generally lit up like day with star shells, and one feels quite uncomfortable when on the parapet at night, even back in these support trenches. The shells are rather interesting from a speculative point of view, for one can hear the heavy ones come whistling very slowly (compara-tively) through the air, and in a very short time one gets very canny and it is possible to estimate very shrewdly where the brute is going to land, and if necessary duck behind a traverse, if there is one . . .'

'*4 July*. The little village which we are fortifying has been fairly blown to bits and not a single house remains. It is in a commanding position. All the trees are cut about and trenches run through streets and gardens, causing a most desolate and forlorn-looking place. We live in dugouts in a sunken road and to all intents and purposes safe from the attentions of brother Boche.

'My work has now switched from these defences to defences in and about the "front line" or "firing-line". It is somewhat awe-inspiring to approach this portion of the line as an absolute greenhorn—and I am quite open to confess I don't feel alto-gether at home there even now. I suppose the trouble is the absolutely unseen danger, and the uncertainty as to where it will come from. Although the opposing trenches are only about 80 to 100 yards away, and the advance posts are only about 10 to 12 yards separated, yet the Boche is an animal of unknown characteristics, which is never seen unless it be under military escort at Le Havre or some other military town. All that shows the nasty beast is in existence is the whizz and bang of the shells and trench mortars which he sends over; of the beast himself there is never a sign.

'This is a particularly noted locality which used to be held by the French. They left 70,000 of their dead behind, some still unburied and I daresay the Germans for their part did not come off scot-free. We often dig into the old birds, and use them for revetting. No one thinks about these sort of sentimentalities out here, although in some respects very great and deep feeling is displayed. I suppose no one who has not been out here can realise quite what a life we lead, or appreciate the humours and annoyances of the daily occurrences. The filth and squalor of the front line trenches, men and all that appertains to them, has to be seen to be imagined, and yet 12 hours after the men are relieved they are as happy as sandboys and clean as new pins.'

'*11 July*. If you wish to get a real impression of the trenches as they really are, you should make a close study of "Bairnsfather's Fragments from France". They are very real. I always thought they were more or less farcical, but they are, I find, a very vivid representation of the real thing. I saw a true Bairnsfather's man the other day and the likeness was so great that another fellow and myself sat down in the mud and fairly screamed with laughter. The man was one of the Royal Scots, with about 2 weeks' growth of beard, dirty as a sweep, plastered with mud, smoking a little "cuttie" pipe, tin hat on, bloodshot eyes, be-kilted with muddy sacking, up to his eyes in treacly mud, and carrying on his back an enormous sack. He didn't seem at all annoyed at our yells of merriment and, in fact, he must have been quite a humorous fellow.

'By heavens though, these Scotties are the finest fellows I have ever had the pleasure of meeting anywhere. Good luck to them wherever they go. They leave this line today and our Cockneys, as they call us, take over instead. The Jocks took over this line from the French about 4 months ago, and they have done fine work here since. The German miners and snipers have been properly mastered, the trenches consolidated and the Hun is generally fairly cowed. Of course there is plenty of strafing still going on, but we appear to give him double the doses he gives us.

'You would never believe the appalling amount of mud there is in the trenches. We had a very heavy rain 2 days ago and hey presto we were knee deep in liquid mud and water. I never used to believe the yarns about standing knee deep in water for weeks at a time but I haven't the SMALLEST doubt about the truth of these tales now. I would like you to see the fellows in the trenches. The dirt and filth is simply indescribable. No one realises how admirable these wonderful infantry are. They are the people who have to do all the work, have to live in the trenches, have to DO the scrapping, and have to BE scrapped, and who are generally the real heroes of this war. They may not be very intelligent on the average but, ye gods, what a life they lead!

'Can you picture it? I'm quite sure that unless you've seen the reality you can have *no conception* of what these wonderful infantry have to put up with. Wet to the skin, in perpetual danger from shells and mortars, mud absolutely all over them, uninteresting work to do, miles of these damnable trenches to carry even the food they eat through, packed like sardines into filthy dugouts down the steps of which mud and water fairly cascade in bad weather, continual repairs to trenches as they get blown in . . . Never despise the Infantryman for he is the most uncomplaining sufferer in this wretched war. Our fellows and we officers have an absolute picnic compared to them.'

'*16 July*. I went up into a saphead situated on a huge mine crater and had a good look round. Brother Boche can, from all

127

visible indications, be only a myth. Isn't it astounding, here are miles of trenches, populated by scores of thousands of men, and yet one cannot see a living soul.

'It is really very astonishing the spirit in which things are taken (and given) out here. For instance yesterday some shrapnel burst just at the proper height and direction over a man's head in a trench, and the bits whizzed all round him. He simply ran down the trench for cover, laughing for all he was worth at the "b——y near one" as he called it. It's always the same with everyone; provided the thing doesn't hit you, it is regarded as a joke . . .

'There is a very fine feeling of comradeship out here, both amongst the men and officers, and one really feels quite a little touch of pride every time one slides round these bally old trenches. Damn funny thing, patriotism, isn't it! Did I tell you of that most pathetic and touching incident of the aged French woman who strewed the road with flowers and sweet herbs for our fellows to march on when we had that long trek? . . .'

'*16 July* . . . Back behind the lines, there are, except for quantities of khaki, no indications of the biggest strafe the world has ever known. The land is tilled up to say $1\frac{1}{2}$ miles of the firing line, and in many cases within 1,000 yards. Civilians still eke out an existence in houses well within the range of rifle bullets, and in houses that are pitted all over with shrapnel bullets.

'Up to the present we have had only one casualty, and he was one of the poor boys in my section. He got shrapnel through the chest. It seems to me that it's all a case of luck out here, and the chap who crawls about a trench on his hands and knees stands as much chance of being snuffed out as the man who doesn't care a jot . . .'

'*20 July*. First we will deal with business. Imagine my unutterable consternation and perturbation of spirit on finding at least one precious lb of my parcel occupied by that appalling species of confectionery known as "bulls-eyes". My dear old

Mater, don't you remember that these things, peppermints, ginger bread, ginger cake and so on, are my particular abomination? The ginger-biscuits, however, were so beautifully crisp and in such good condition that I must fain confess that I do not absolutely dislike them. In fact, I might even say they are rather nice!

'The cake was absolute perfection! I shouldn't make them very MUCH plainer however. Don't send tobacco or candles as we can buy them. Cut out the matches, as the petrol lighter is very good. A *Sunday Times* would be very acceptable once a week. Send some good thick plain writing paper. Those crested envelopes are useless, as we are not allowed to use them. You might send 1 bottle or jar of bloater paste once per 3 weeks . . .'

'*24 July* . . . The bombardment I mentioned was really only a trivial affair compared with the stunt down south, but it was a sufficiently impressive sight for anyone fresh from England. The whole business is conducted in a very cool and premeditated sort of way which one can hardly associate with war as one fondly imagines it. Programmes are printed and circulated to those concerned, showing times and details of the various phases of the strafe. At the appointed time precisely, the strafe commences, generally with a sort of "feeler" in the way of a few dozen trench mortars, or "Minnies" as we sometimes call them, and perhaps a stiffening of whizz-bangs (field gun shells).

'After, say, precisely 22 minutes, an intense "hate" is transmitted for the space say of $2\frac{1}{2}$ minutes, through the medium of every bally projectile that can be scraped together and heaved across by every available gun in the section, as well as perhaps a suspicion of seasoning from an aeroplane gun, to make the consignment more palatable. Suddenly then there is an absolute cessation of fire for a few minutes, then up the music starts again, with perhaps a soft accompaniment of smoke fuses coloured green to imitate the dreaded "gas" which fairly puts the "wind up" Brother Boche. After a stanza to this strain, we may hand over a concentrated dose of shrapnel, hoping to catch Huns outside their dugouts, and keep this up for say 5 minutes.

'Then a few more salvos from "Minnies" and the show is over, when we (the interested spectators) walk back to tea from the specially selected "seats" in the support lines of the trenches, laughing and joking over what has occurred just as if it were a "show" in one of the London theatres.

'At the same time the Boche crawl out of their dugouts where they have been safely ensconced and swear vigorously as they survey the considerable amount of damage done, and think of all the extra fatigues which will be required before things are put right again. He then returns to his dugouts to wait till dark and works out schemes of super-retaliation in the meantime.

'About 15 to 20 miles south, however, it is quite a different story. There we can hear a terrible roar of guns which has lasted now without cessation ever since we have been here, nearly 5 weeks, except for small intervals amounting to not more than 7 days. From here we can see the dull red flash of the explosions, see the sky lit up with star shells, and on still nights feel the ground quivering even here. One fails to conceive how flesh and blood can stand the strain. There we have no fine dugouts, no snug billets, but are open to all this awful hell of shell fire.

'When one realises that this gross expenditure is necessary in order to *win back* only a paltry 5 × 2 miles of territory, it is hard to imagine the days when our armies drive the Hun back to their own country again. Personally I feel sure they never will come, on this side at least. I am not a pessimist, but on the other hand one would be foolish not to look things squarely in the face.'

'*19 August* . . . A few days ago there was a bombing raid on a certain bit of Boche line and about 40 men participated. They got it in the neck practically as soon as they got over their own parapet, but plugged manfully on, practised "frightfulness" to a considerable extent on the Hun in his own dugouts where he had taken refuge or was caught napping, through the persuasive influence of stink bombs, explosive bombs and bayonets, and then returned to their own lines, quite pleased with life in general. Men were hit, but went on, were hit again and went on, some were wounded in 13 or 14 places and one had 40 wounds and yet went on, till loss of blood weakened him too much.

'The party lost its way when coming back and up to 2 days afterwards men were rescued from no man's land in pairs and 3s and 4s refusing to leave one another and tending to one another's wounds. One man's life was unquestionably saved through the care and devotion of his comrade, who carried him into a shell hole where he stayed during 24 hours looking after his wounded comrade like a mother, and he eventually guided a stretcher party to the spot . . .'

'*19 August* [to his uncle]. I hope that by now you have finished hay-making and made a good start with the harvesting. It is an inspiring sight to see the aged men, women and children harvesting the corn out here with any old machines or scythes that have escaped the general wreckage. All along the line the crops are being grown within one or two miles of the front trenches, where of course shells could easily reach the harvesters. How long do you expect this rotten business to last? The whole thing is thoroughly unsporting and you may get a faint idea of one feature of this stunt when I tell you that I haven't seen a single Hun since I have been out here except as a prisoner-of-war, although no doubt if I took the trouble to wait and watch with glasses I might see one, at least his head and shoulders, walking down a trench . . .'

'*16 September* . . . Some harassed infantry men were talking the other day and one said "B—— fine life this army, ain't it." "Yes, rotten lot of b——s; in England you hear nothing but ' 'Old yer 'ead up, 'old yer 'ead up' and out 'ere it's nothing else but 'Keep yer 'ead down, keep yer 'ead down'—wot are yer going to do?" . . .'

'*1 October*. We had rather an interesting little bet with the Brigade the other day, to the effect that 3 officers of this company would dig a given size rectangular hole deeper in a given time than would 3 officers selected from the Infantry. The wager was a "wee drappie" labelled Johnny Walker. We sallied forth with the two rival teams armed to the teeth with gas helmets and 2 picks and 2 shovels. The rectangles were laid out with great accuracy, 5' × 2', and on the given signal we leapt into the task. The digging was arranged so that each man worked at top speed for two minutes and then recovered his breath during a pause of four minutes. One could hardly see the work progressing amidst the clouds of flying earth and steam, but at the tick of 30 minutes work we were stopped, and after the earth was cool enough to touch, the depths were sounded with the minutest accuracy, while the spectators proceeded to make friends with the likely winners. After measuring and remeasuring for several minutes the judges awarded us the prize, by a margin of 2". The total volume excavated was about 30 cubic feet . . .'

Case's mole-like existence on the Western Front was nearing an end. The skills he had learned during his year's engineering training had been put to constant use. Now, for the last two years of the war in Macedonia, Egypt and Palestine, he was to be mostly in the open, employed in a variety of tasks from the building (and demolition) of bridges and roads to the laying-on of water supplies for an army surrounded by desert. He was to end the war as he had begun it, on horseback—but a horse used merely for mobility, the jeep of World War I.

A volume of letters covers this period, but though they include appalled descriptions of the savage fighting in Palestine in 1917 (when mounted Yeomanry regiments came at last into their own), it is evident that it was in the trenches of Flanders that he glimpsed the ultimate horror of war.

His abhorrence at the senseless slaughter is given full vent in one of his last letters from the trenches, a letter that reveals how complete had become his disillusionment since those euphoric early days of the war, when the call to arms had seemed no more than a 'Tally-ho' to some great sporting adventure.

'*20 October* . . . One would hardly believe the extraordinary audacity of the rats out here. They almost eat the clothes off one's back, and hardly take the trouble to get out of one's way when walking along a trench. I saw a very interesting sight the other day when walking along the trench. Something flashed round the corner of a traverse and on investigation it proved to be a tiny little baby weasel carrying along a half-grown rat which it had apparently killed. I followed it along for nearly 50 yards when, with prodigious efforts, the little beast actually carried the rat up over the side of the trench. The pluck and marvellous energy of the little weasel pleased me immensely but I couldn't help contrasting his mode of life to our own.

'Here are we, the most cultivated nations upon earth (as we smugly imagine ourselves) waging the dirtiest and most unsporting warfare that could possibly be imagined, hiding in holes and ditches, throwing at one another the most appalling types of HE with sometimes the most dreadful consequences, and not even seeing the persons who are blown up, and here was this primitive little beast waging a truly sporting healthy warfare in single-handed fight against a foe as strong as himself.

'The very thought of this warfare makes one absolutely sick and disgusted. Look at it, HE, gas, flammenwerfer, machineguns, poisoned water, mines—hardly a single filthy underhand means of offence has been omitted. The latest addition is the phosphorous bomb, and I suppose it is only a matter of time and we shall be spraying concentrated sulphuric acid at one another. I only wonder it's not been resorted to before . . .'

6 *Intrepid Birdman*

'. . . The machine-gun fire from the ground is pretty awful. You
see the old Huns crouching in the trenches and they "crack-
crack-crack" at you for all they're worth. Then the sight of our
Tommies relieves you and you know you're out of Hunland . . .'

To the fighter pilot on the Western Front the war was a
totally different experience from that of the soldier in the
trenches. 'Hunland' was not that quickly taken glimpse of
barbed wire and earthworks, splintered trees and ruined build-
ings, menacing across the shell-pocked morass of no man's land,
but just another part of the countryside casually peered down
on from an open cockpit. And usually less to be feared than
the ack-ack shells and bullets coming up from it were the enemy
fighters swooping from the encircling sky.

The letters that nineteen-year-old Lieutenant Yvone Kirkpatrick wrote to his parents from France during the last six
months of the war come from a different world to that described
by young army officers like Lieutenant Case. Couched in jaunty
schoolboy language ('A great scrap', 'pretty exciting', 'rather
good sport'), the immediate impression they give is that the
war in the air was all a bit of a lark. And in Kirkpatrick's few
references to the land fighting there is an air of clinical detachment that seems to border on the callous: 'When we've dropped
our bombs we career about the battlefield. It's awfully interest-

ing and I really enjoy it. You see all sorts of things—burnt out
tanks, Huns hanging up to dry in barbed wire etc . . .'

But that Kirkpatrick was fairly typical of the eager young
'intrepid birdmen' urgently recruited at that time, and was by
no means the callow youth some of the letters may seem to
indicate, is apparent from the diaries and letters of other pilots,
and from the commentary to the letters he is able to provide
today, looking back at the age of seventy-five to the most
eventful months of his life.

The fatalistic attitude to death, the laconic language in which
the grimmest experiences are related, were an instinctive reflex
to the almost daily risk of being shot in flames from the sky
(Battle of Britain pilots, talking of 'wizard prangs', showed much
the same morale-boosting flippancy). But above all it was the
pilot's remoteness from the realities of trench warfare that conditioned his reactions. 'Really you know when we're on the
ground it's more like a summer holiday than a war,' Kirkpatrick writes from the idyllic billet set in an orchard to which
he flew back from his daily sorties over Hunland. 'We just sit
under the trees and read and smoke.'

At his home at Wimborne Minster, Dorset, a few miles from
Canford School where he spent the last thirty-three years of his
career as a schoolmaster, Kirkpatrick can still clearly call to
mind that feeling of isolation from the mainstream of the war.

'We had very little idea of what the infantry man was going
through, though we knew it was absolute hell. From the air you
saw very little of it. By comparison we were living in very great
comfort. But we did not feel in any way guilty. Everyone knew
how short was the life-expectancy of a pilot. If we met soldiers
on a day's leave in St Omer or Boulogne we were treated as
rather glamorous figures, but they didn't envy us at all. Their
attitude was "Sooner you than me!" '

At the time he joined the Royal Flying Corps in May 1917,
Kirkpatrick describes himself as 'a very ordinary conventional
public school boy going to do what I had always wanted to do

—fly'. Eldest of a family of four living at Blackheath, London, his father was Chief Engineer for the Port of London Authority. From his mother he inherited a love of music (his letters have a number of references to classical records he has acquired or wants), and from both parents a strict moral code (the 'eat, drink and be merry' philosophy of some pilots was not for him).

The inspiration behind his ambition to fly was an 1843 colour print (hanging today over his study mantlepiece) that depicts *Ariel*, a steam-engined monoplane, airborne over Hampstead Heath, to the evident astonishment and delight of onlookers. Though a flight of the imagination, the fact that it was his great-grandfather, Frederick Marriott, who had played a leading part in the creation of the actual *Ariel* (still to be seen in the Science Museum) had fired his boyish imagination.

At Shrewsbury School, where his academic record had been undistinguished and cross-country running had been the only sport in which he had made any mark, a visiting RFC officer's recruiting talk to the Officers' Training Corps had only served to reinforce his eagerness to join the select ranks of the intrepid birdmen. He would have enlisted in 1916 had his father given his sanction.

The Royal Flying Corps (to be renamed the Royal Air Force shortly before Kirkpatrick reached the Western Front in May 1918) had changed out of all recognition since the first days of the war when a pioneer band of little over a hundred officers had hazarded their 'stick-and-string' flying machines in the skies over Mons. Though the wooden-framed machines were still primitive by World War II standards, they were now playing an important and varied role, with bombing and photographic aircraft penetrating deep inside enemy territory, two-seaters registering for the artillery behind the German lines, and single-seater fighters on constant 'offensive patrols'—tactical bombing raids, harassment of troops and transport, shooting down observation balloons, engaging enemy aircraft in dog-fights of mounting ferocity.

Kirkpatrick was surprised at the interest shown by the Imperial War Museum after they had come to hear of the collection of typescript copies of over 100 of his letters preserved by his parents, and asked if they could be added to their archives. He had not been one of those (like Case) who wrote letters from the front in carefully worded, semi-diary style, with an eye to posterity. Quite the reverse. 'What a funny idea to get all my letters typewritten,' he wrote to his father from France. 'I don't mind so long as they are confined to the family, but if I get done in for heaven's sake don't go and publish them in *Comic Cuts* or *Nash's Magazine* like some people have done.'

That these letters were dashed off with no thought of ever being read outside the family circle gives them a frankness and sense of immediacy that more than compensates for any lack of literary quality. Alternating between the breathless and the blasé, one is constantly aware that Kirkpatrick is still little more than a boy, fresh from the inhibiting confines of an élite boarding-school. 'Ripping', 'topping' and 'jolly' are favourite adjectives, and a tendency to show off indicates his eagerness to prove himself in an adult world.

In a yearly record his mother kept of her children's progress, she describes Yvone in 1917 as having shown at school 'not enough hard concentrated work or ambition' but as being 'a charming person to look at and to live with—everyone loves him'. His ambition to fly at last realised, his early letters are redolent with the excitement of being set free into a man's world. Recalling today the first three months of training, devoted to an infantry course, Kirkpatrick says: 'The discipline was very strict, the drilling, lectures and exams gruelling, but I was much happier than at Shrewsbury.'

Simply to be airborne was something to write home about at a time when aviation was still in its infancy and 'intrepid bird-man' a phrase not yet outdated. During the intensive flying course on which Kirkpatrick embarked after passing his exams and obtaining his commission in August 1917, the trainee had to accustom himself to risks and discomforts quite unknown to pilots of the streamlined Spitfires and Hurricanes of the last war. The flying machine of World War I had an open cockpit, no heating and no oxygen for flying at freezing altitudes, no retractable undercarriage or brakes for landing, no radio links with other aircraft or ground staff, and (by an official ruling that was later to be denounced as having caused the needless deaths of hundreds of pilots) no parachutes were worn.

The Sopwith Camel to which Kirkpatrick graduated was easily the most successful British fighter on the Western Front, but also the most treacherous to handle. Among trainees the rate of casualties, often fatal, was high, from uncontrollable spins, crashes on landing, mid-air collisions during mock combats. In describing his first solo flight, on 26 August, Kirkpatrick mentions almost casually that he had hit a plane (wing) on landing, adding that 'the average for a solo flight is generally the undercarriage or a plane or two'.

The severity of the training methods is hinted at in his reference to the instructor in one dual-control flight—'He shouts and hits you about a good deal in the air but I am beginning to think he is not such a bad instructor after all.' There is scarcely a grouse or grumble in his letters home. And near the end of the course, with the Allied armies reeling back from the Germans' 'Big Push' in the spring of 1918 and replacements urgently needed as pilot casualties soared, he is more eager than ever to get into the fight. An added inspiration is the presence of two veteran fighter pilots, both VCs, recalled as instructors to speed the flow: Colonel Rees ('awful sportsman, brought down 3 Huns and drove off 2 when he'd got an explosive bullet in his leg so that he could only control the machine with the other leg') and Major McCudden, one of the great air aces of the war, who is lecturing on 'How to bring Huns down'.

Extracts from five of the fifty-one letters Kirkpatrick wrote to

his parents and sister during his year's training in various parts
of the country will suffice to indicate the eagerness with which
he took to the air. They make an intriguing contrast with the
1915 letters of Trooper Case describing the hazards of horsemanship. The war that had started with an implicit belief in the
importance of mounted troops was to end with recognition of
an airforce as something more than an adjunct to the army: a
service in its own right.

'*24 July 1917*, Fort Rowner, Gosport. I am having an absolutely ripping time here and I simply love flying. We went
down to the 'drome and our instructor took us each up for about
seven minutes and did various stunts to see how we liked it. It's
simply fine; you climb in through a network of wires and sit in
a topping little seat with a set of controls in front of you and the
pilot in front. He yells out "Contact", the mechanic buzzes the
propeller round and she starts. First of all you go bumping
over the grass for about 150 yards, then he pulls back the control
lever and up she goes over some trees.

'It's fine when you look down on houses and people, everything looks quite ordinary though, just like from a high building. You get a fine view from here. If you look at the map you
will see that the Solent is in front and Portsmouth harbour
behind. Well, soon we were quite high over the Solent, about
1,000 feet, you can see people bathing and all the ships look
ripping. The old *Aquitania* is out in the Solent and she looks fine.
Round we went again, back over the land into the aerodrome.
He switched off the engine till it was just ticking over and
glided down and landed without a bump.

'Flying gives you that ripping feeling like skiing; in fact it's
jolly like skiing except that you get a much nicer view. When he
switch-backed it gives you that sinking feeling that you get at
the White City, only more so. If you can imagine a compound
of skiing, motoring and switch-backing you might have some
idea what flying feels like, only nothing could describe how
lovely the sun and sea and everything looks . . .

139

'Today I took the controls. Then after breakfast I was up again and this time I did straights and turns by myself; somehow it seems jolly easy. We went a long way out over the sea and we saw an old seaplane lumbering along below us, so the pilot signed me to let my control go slack and down we shot until we were just over the seaplane and we had a good look into his "office". He had a terrific paraphernalia of maps, wireless etc and we followed him for quite a long way, then up we shot again, then he signed me to do some banks which I did. The first one was a bit too steep because I was rather too sudden with the controls, but when we came down he said the last two were jolly good. We did a great bank round Lee-on-Solent Pier and you could see funny white blobs looking up from the beach that were faces. I expect I will be doing landings soon, they are the hardest part but all you need is practice . . .'

'*3 March 1918*, [to his sister Lettice, a boarder at Wycombe Abbey School] Market Drayton . . . I am flying Sopwith Pups now, ripping little single-seater scouts, and I go diving at barnyard fowls and pigs and people round Market Drayton. I haven't had a chance to stunt one yet as the clouds have been too low. They are much faster than Avros and do about 110 mph level! . . .

'No flappers here at all! If you've got any pretty ones who want to waste time writing to "an intrepid birdman" by all means ask them, photos enclosed if poss. As you know my taste is very particular! Yours till H——L freezes . . .'

'*4 March*. Yesterday five of us did a formation for 1 hr 50 mins on end and got absolutely lost. All I know is that we went from here to Chester, back over the aerodrome, round Shrewsbury, on again past Chester, and then I think we wandered all over Lancashire and back over Crewe, over the Potteries and eventually picked up the canal and saw a Very light which they were firing to attract our attention. The clouds were very low and we were at about 1,000 feet most of the time. One of the formation left us near Liverpool and was last seen going due north at about 120 mph. He's not been heard of since.

'A few days ago one of our fellows had a forced landing at the Countess of Warwick's place near Chester. A footman came out and asked him what they could do and this fellow Secombe was very surprised to find where he'd landed. Two girls came along and he asked who they were. He was told they were the Princesses of Teck! The wretched fellow was in a terrible state as he didn't know how to address them. Then there were two very pretty girls, daughters of the Countess, Lady Ursula and Lady Somebodyelse. Apparently he got awfully mixed up with calling them "My Lady Ursula" and "Your Highness" and "Your Majesty" etc! However they were very decent to him and the butler produced a pair of silk pyjamas belonging to the old boy, who, I understand, doesn't live with them. They gave him champagne dinners etc, and he only had a very dirty uniform on and no razor. The silly fool was in too much of a panic to get the footman or somebody to find him a razor. Altogether he had 3 days there. Then they came and repaired his bus and the Major flew it back . . .'

'*1 April*. I love a Camel now but I don't take liberties with it near the ground. It proves conclusively that if a man like Booth who must have done 100 hours on Camels—he brought down 7 Huns in France—can't do what he likes with a Camel every time near the ground, nobody else can. He started a spin at about 600 feet this morning and went straight into the ground "Splash". I won't go into the details, but he wasn't much like a human being when I saw him. The snaps I took of the Camel's remains will give you some idea how bad it was. It was absolutely in splinters to about half way down the tail . . .'

'*14 April*, Turnberry, Scotland [after describing how, on a solo flight, he had encountered a Bristol monoplane—unbeknown to him piloted by the Station Commandant, Colonel Rees, VC—and engaged it in a lively chase]. When I came down I found that the people in the sheds had been watching us and they said I had much the best of the fight. About five minutes later along came the Colonel and asks my Flight Commander who was in the Sopwith Camel NB 7416; so Elliott told him that a man by the name of Kirkpatrick was in it, so along comes the Colonel looking for Kirkpatrick. When he found me he said "I was in the Bristol monoplane." I nearly fell backwards with surprise. However, he was awfully bucked and said it was a jolly good scrap and I did very well as he couldn't shake me off and I had much more speed and power than he did. Everybody was awfully amused as it's not every day you get the chance of chasing VC, MC colonels about the atmosphere . . .'

When Kirkpatrick reached France, on 2 May 1918, a lull had set in after the bitter fighting that had raged since Ludendorff launched his all-out offensive on 21 March. The German attempt to separate the French and British, to take the Channel ports and destroy the British army (at the height of which Haig had issued his famous 'Backs to the wall' order of the day) had failed, but at a terrible cost. In the bloodiest forty days' fighting of the war there had been nearly 240,000 British casualties.

In preparation for their offensive, the Germans had greatly increased their output of aircraft and trained pilots, and the final battle for air supremacy had now developed, with patrols of from twenty to fifty enemy fighters a not uncommon sight over the Allied lines. Casualty figures had soared on both sides and it was generally accepted that a fighter pilot new to the Front would be lucky if his name had not appeared in a casualty list within three or four weeks.

Though Kirkpatrick saw friends killed and himself had frequent narrow escapes, his letters maintain a buoyant note to the end. What particularly strikes one today is his consistently bloodthirsty attitude to 'the Hun'. Even on Armistice Day he is regretting a patrol over the confused front the day before when he failed to shoot up a cartload of soldiers later identified as German ('I did feel mad, especially as my guns were going so

well that morning'). Such an attitude had to a large extent been
conditioned during four years of war on the Home Front, where
hatred of the Hun was seen as a patriotic duty and had been
fanned to a new hysteria by the intensified air raids of 1917.

Kirkpatrick's most chilling description is of a German pilot
'done to a frazzle' after being shot down in flames. That there
was nothing gloating about this is apparent from his recollections today of the many dog-fights in which he took part.
'There was more of mutual respect than hatred between opposing pilots. Aerial warfare was a very impersonal thing—you
didn't feel you were shooting down a man, it was your machine
against someone else's. If we had shot down a German pilot
alive our side of the lines we would probably have brought him
into the Mess and treated him as one of ourselves. And we
would have expected to have been treated the same his side of
the lines.'

Until mid-October, when the war had developed into a confused harassment of the rapidly retreating enemy, Kirkpatrick
was stationed with 203 Squadron at Izel le Hameau in open
countryside some ten miles west of Arras. This was known
throughout the RAF as a paradise of a billet, set in the orchard
of a former chateau, now a farm. The airfield was an extensive
plateau flanked by wooded slopes where hutments provided
permanent accommodation for three squadrons. Earlier occu-
pants had built a comfortable officers' mess, with bar and large
brick fireplace. There were ample recreational facilities, including a tennis court and regular cinema shows. And reclining
on hot days in the shade of the orchard, with nothing more
sinister to be heard than the drone of bees and whine of
mosquitos, the war going on over the horizon could seem in
another world.

The basic comforts of life at Izel le Hameau are indicated by
the extra items Kirkpatrick asks to be sent from home. To the
soldier enduring the primitive conditions of the trenches they
would have seemed the height of luxury: 'a tin of 100 HAND

MADE "Three Castles" Virginian—one gets rather fed up with Turkish always': 'one of those big tins of Mackintosh's "Mint de Luxe"—I'm getting fed up with chocolate and we can get tons of it here now'. A steady flow of books came from home, titles he mentions including *The Man Eaters of Tsavo* ('jolly interesting'), Masefield's *Multitude and Solitude* ('too gloomy'), Stackpole's *Children of the Sea* ('very morbid, lots of leprosy in it!'). His one deprivation was classical music. The pop records of the day were preferred by the Squadron which was mostly composed of colonials.

Kirkpatrick's descriptions of offensive patrols and dog-fights have a fearless, sometimes exultant ring to them, but it is evident that back at base there was little of the hell-raiser in his makeup. On short leaves in St Omer and Boulogne he preferred 'sitting in a teashop eating ices, strawberries and fruit salad, or in cafés on the boulevard drinking grenadines and watching the people go by', to the riotous parties in which many of his brother officers indulged. He mentions that he is thinking of taking up Pelmanism 'just for something to do', though it is not boredom he is referring to when he later writes: 'It's simply awful the amount of sleep we get.' Sleep was nature's answer to the mounting strain of combat, the exhaustion that followed exposure to high altitudes in an open cockpit, the bottled-up emotions as another friend failed to return from Hunland.

The war was to turn out differently in many respects from his preconceptions, but there was nothing but elation in his heart when at last he landed in France. After a week's impatient waiting, he learned that he was being posted to 203 Squadron and wrote jubilantly home: ' "Gloria in excelsis deo" or in other words "thumbs up!!" '

'*19 May*, Izel le Hameau. Well, this place is absolutely topping. Our quarters are in an orchard, and there's plenty of shade and green grass with an old horse on it. As I got here before the others I managed to bag a decent hut with wallpaper on the walls and linoleum on the floor, bookcases, cupboards, a table, electric light, and a fair sprinkling of fair maidens on the wall who look, by their attire, as if "La Vie Parisienne" was a pretty warm place. However, they are better than nothing, and the cunning merchant who stuck them up has stuck up lots of "Old Bills" out of *The Bystander* amongst them, giving them the glad eye . . .

'Yesterday morning I went up and had a look at the Great War for the first time. You see, it was like this. I asked the CO if I could take a machine up for a flip and he said "Yes alright, you'd better go with Captain Little and he'll show you the lines." So I went along and Capt Little said he and another fellow were going up to hunt for Hun 2-seaters and if I liked I could come along with them; so I went. We met one Hun, only he was so well camouflaged we lost him and he buzzed off east. Once I thought we had one. Little gave the "Hun sign" by wobbling his machine from side to side, and then he did a sort of "cart-wheel" to the right, and I went over after him and saw a 2-seater some way below. When we got down we found it was one of our machines, so we pushed off. We were up at 13,000 feet and you could see a good deal of smashed country but you couldn't tell what was our present line . . .

'By the way I forgot to tell you a tale about Captain Little. Just before he went home on leave he was so badly shot up by the Huns that his machine fell to pieces at 10,000 feet and he came down in a nose dive, but at about 20 feet off the ground it zoomed up and the fuselage fell in half and he fell out and landed in a ploughed field unhurt! This was in no man's land by the way. Then a Hun came and fired at him from his machine, so old Little pulled out a revolver and shot at him. Then, tonight, he came down apparently out of control, right on to an Archie (anti-aircraft gun) battery, and then pulled himself together and dived on them, firing both guns. They were so surprised that they left their guns and ran away down a street . . .'

145

'*27 May*. I've been over the lines four times now and started to go with the flight on a regular show last night. The second time was with a fellow called Webster. We were told to go and see if we could find any fat old 2-seaters this side of the lines. We went up the lines, climbing the whole time, and when we got to the far end we were at 18,000 ft. I didn't notice it much, the only effect it had on me was to make me imagine that every bus I saw was a Hun. It was very clear and you could see England (the south coast and the Thames estuary) quite clearly, also Holland. Blighty looked a long way away, but we were a fair way from the French coast.

'Well, I don't know where we went quite, but this fellow wanted to show me what Archie was like, so he took me over a famous Archie battery, but they never noticed us, we were so high. We saw 8 Huns quite close, but didn't go after them as we were on the other side of the lines. They were apparently trying to make us think there was a scrap going on by the way they were fooling about and trying to entice us into it. Of course, if we'd gone and had a look they'd have all been after us.

'The next show I did was one evening we went over to drop bombs in certain places and then come down and fire our machine-guns at the Hun trenches. Well, I got my bombs off alright and then we started going round a wood and diving at these Huns. After I'd done about half a dozen dives my engine started to miss on one cylinder, so I thought it about time to come home, and duly pointed my nose west and made off. I was pretty low and I couldn't recognise anything, and after about five minutes my engine stopped altogether, so I decided to land in a big field which looked all right. When I got to it I found it was downhill with plough at the bottom with the result that as soon as I got to the plough my bus turned upside down. It was quite comfortable for me but smashed up all four planes. I then proceeded to turn the petrol off and get out.

'Fortunately there were some ASC people near and they put a guard over it, and put me up for the night, and the next morning a tender took me back, and a lorry took the bus back. I found that the engine, a new one to me, had seized up owing partly to the heat and partly to the way I was running it. You have to be awfully careful not to give these engines too much petrol, which I had subconsciously done.

'Last night we went up on a high op up and down our bit of the lines. We didn't see any Huns but we got plenty of old Krupps' fireworks chucked at us. It's rather amusing being Archie'd, personally I didn't mind this stuff, I had the wind up about my engine. I thought it was going to do the same as it did the last time, as it wasn't going well. Archie appeared to me like this [sketch]. Suddenly I heard a sort of cr-r-r-rump and looked over and saw a black cloud on my left, then another one behind, then we turned and he left us alone. I wouldn't mind being Archie'd all day and night if it got no nearer than that . . .

'I was very busy yesterday putting up electric light in my hut and now it's quite hot stuff. Really you know when we're on the ground it's more like a summer holiday than a war. We just sit under the trees and read and smoke. The food, well it's superlative. I don't want to make your mouth water, but we have cream, butter and eggs off the farm! In the evening we either go rat-hunting with revolvers, rifles, sticks and electric torches, or go to the pictures! The other squadron has a fine cinema show every evening with an orchestra and jolly good pictures, supplied by the Expeditionary Force Canteen, and the officers pay 1 franc a time. This last week we've had a theatre as well. One of our hangars has a stage and the 13th Btn of Canadians have been giving variety performances. They are jolly good and two of their men make jolly good girls. One is so good in fact that one of our officers wouldn't believe he was a man and wanted to be introduced! . . .'

'*29 May* . . . After an air raid last night, Capt Little, the temporary CO, went up after them in a Camel but apparently the old Hun got the better of it as he was found dead this morning about 50 km away. He apparently was wounded and

147

fainted and then crashed. It's jolly bad luck on him too, he'd brought down umpteen Huns and had the DSO and bar, DSC and bar and the Croix de Guerre. He was an awfully good fellow, an Australian, and we used to go ratting with him at night . . .'

Routine offensive patrols, often twice daily, and increasing entanglements with enemy fighters form the burden of the remainder of Kirkpatrick's letters and there is inevitably an element of repetitiveness about them. Extracts with some particular point of general interest have here been selected, together with occasional references to camp life.

'*5 June*. Last night's op was rather nice. There were clouds at about 1,500 ft, thick with an occasional hole here and there. As there was nothing doing down below we went up on top. It was so strange coming out of the damp murky stuff below to the gorgeous blue sky and brilliant white on the top of the clouds. They seemed so solid and looked just like I should imagine the North Pole looks like, with chasms and hills and all sorts of things. We went up to 14,000 ft and then got fed up again and spotted a hole and dived through. I was flying on the right tail of the formation as usual and it was so funny to see the formation going down, simply tumbling over themselves to get through the hole. We were diving at about 200 mph for about 8,000 ft I should think . . .'

'*11 June* . . . I've acquired a dog now. It's a queer sandy coloured sort of hound. It turned up here looking half-starved, with some nasty sores on its legs, which looked as if it had been caught in a trap, so I've fed it up and it's beginning to cheer up now. I don't think it's got much sense, it seems to do nothing but sleep and eat. I think it must have botulism . . .'

'*21 June* . . . I haven't flown at night and I don't want to either; the nearest approach was the dawn patrol at 4 am the other morning. You could only just see one or two stars in the west then, and it was pretty dark, just light enough to see to take off. I should imagine the stars at night look just the same as they do from a mountain . . . Oh, by the way, I'm going to study Pelmanism just for something to do, so probably my income will treble and I'll end up a field marshal in the RAF or something . . .'

'*25 June*. It's simply awful the amount of sleep we get. Take yesterday for instance. Op at 4 am, nothing seen except quite an interesting sunrise. Back to bed at 5.45. Up at 8.55 to dash into breakfast in pyjamas, then back to bed. Up at 11. Patrol at 11.30, weather pretty dud, back in the rain. Lunch at 12.30. After lunch lie down and read and sleep till 4.15. After tea get dressed up and go for walk till dinner at 7.30. Then pictures at 8.15–10. Back to bed at 10.30. Called at 6.30 this morning, told there's a patrol at 6.45. "What's the weather like?" "Fine, sir" says the optimistic sentry. "H——L's teeth" remark I. At 6.30 prepare to get up when somebody comes along and says it's getting dud. Cheers, back to bed, patrol eventually washed out, so I settle down and sleep till 8.55, crash in to breakfast, then back to bed . . .

'PS My dog has deserted me, I don't mind much as he was rather a silly looking beast, and he only ate and slept, like me.'

'*29 June*. Yesterday evening we went and had a look at the war at close quarters. I expect you'll see it announced in the papers. Quite a little affair, but we were tootling along at about 100 ft on the other side of the lines, looking for things. When you are down low all the shells that are buzzing about make a beastly noise and you can hear "pop-pop-pop" from the ground, and on the whole it's quite thrilling. I saw a mine or dump or something go up, it looked like a great spout of mud that went up about 100 ft and then flopped down, leaving a lot of smoke behind it . . .'

'*2 July*. I've been having quite an exciting time lately with several scraps. Yesterday morning we came across the other flight having an enormous dog-fight with five Pfalz Scouts, one of which they brought down. We went on a bit when the leader saw a 2-seater down below so he immediately thought he'd go down and put him out of his misery. Just before he dived, however, I remembered the umpteen lectures I'd had on the good old Hun's trick of putting an old 2-seater down below and a few Scouts up in the sun where you can't see them, so I just took a look up and I'm blowed if I didn't see 3 or 4 Pfalz Scouts sitting up there. I wasn't going to dive down too, so I just went over west a bit and climbed up.

'The old Huns didn't notice me apparently, as the first one did a huge turn and dived on our tail man firing at him in great style. However, I got him in my sight and let him have the benefit of my 2 quickfirers for a bit. He just went straight down so I don't know if I got him or not . . .'

'*12 July* [after describing running into a storm] . . . by the time we got home the wind was a hurricane and 3 of us crashed on landing—Titch, Stone and I. Mine was the worst. I made a good landing and before I had stopped a gust of wind blew me round and chucked me on my nose in a very undignified position. My bus unfortunately was badly damaged in its tummy—engine. However, accidents will happen and it might have happened to anyone. Now I'll get another bus. My last one was an absolute beauty and I shall be lucky if the next one is as good.

'The same morning the people in another flight went up after a 2-seater. One of them was Flt Cdr Whealy, who's got a lot of Huns. They spotted the 2-seater and began to approach him with nefarious intentions. No sooner had they begun to attack him than a gutty member of 6 Hun Scouts, which were sitting up above watching, dived down on the other fellow, Hunter, and got behind him and would probably have shot him down if it hadn't been for Whealy who shot the Hun down. They watched him come down and hit the ground this side of the lines and go off with a pop. He burst into flames when he hit the ground. They then returned home feeling very bucked with life. After lunch they decided to go and see if they could collect any relics, so complete with a French map, by which they made out the Hun was about 1,000 yards this side of the lines, they set off with the CO in his car.

'They got on alright and when the ground began to get rough they decided to leave the car and walk. By this time they'd reached the trenches, which they noticed had men in the bottom. However, no one took any notice of them and as there was no war going on they walked quite peacefully along the parapet till they found their Hun. Apparently the machine was a total wreck, and the merchant himself was, as Whealy put it, "Done to a frazzle". I know you all like meaty details. His head was stove in by the guns, and his feet and hands were practically burnt off, also he hadn't a stitch of clothing left on him.

'Well, as they were contemplating him, suddenly a shell burst about five yards off them, then one the other side. By this time they had fallen into the trench and were making off as quick as they could. It appeared that they were only 500 yards from the Hun trenches when they had been examining the old Boche! None of them was hurt, and they all came back looking rather pleased and feeling very glad they weren't in the infantry . . .'

After a brief leave with his family at a Welsh farmhouse, Kirkpatrick got back, on 25 July, to find that he had missed 'a colossal dog-fight in which I would probably have got a Hun. Titch, Stone and 2 others each got a Hun, and Titch saw Rudge on a Hun's tail who went down in flames; but when they got out of it Rudge was missing. Nobody knows what happened to him, but I'm afraid he was done in. I'm awfully sorry as I liked him very much. He'd not been with us very long. He'd been with the RFC in Italy. He was at Paris before the war studying international law and naturally spoke French like a native and he and I always used to go about together on our days off in Boulogne and naturally have a lot of fun . . .'

'*26 July* . . . Brown missing . . . Really B Flight has done awfully well in the last few days in the way of Huns, but it's too bad losing Rudge and Brown. I haven't got over Rudge going west yet. I don't think I've really met anyone I liked or had so much in common with as him since I joined the RFC . . .'

During an air raid on the aerodrome on 31 July Kirkpatrick was slightly injured when a piece of shrapnel gashed his right forearm, and he spent the next six days at a base hospital. He learned that his family had not received his letters from hospital and, after the ominous delivery of an Air Ministry telegram 'regretting to inform them' that he had been wounded, had been in a 'horrible state of wind up'.

The Allied armies were now increasing the pressure that was to erupt in the storming of the 'impregnable' Hindenburg Line on 26 September and the German air force was more active than ever. In hospital Kirkpatrick had learned that something 'pretty exciting' was afoot. 'My word it is nice to get back to the Squadron, it's just like coming home,' he wrote. 'Felt very queer my first flip but quite alright now. Plenty of Huns around —the CO saw 50 in a bunch yesterday.'

On 17 September he had his first close look at the trenches he had so often flown over during the past four months. 'The Huns had only left a few days before and I collected quite a lot of interesting souvenirs, of which this is the list; 1 Hun rifle and bayonet (brand new nearly), 1 Hun gas mask, 1 camouflaged Hun tin helmet, 1 lock of Hun machine gun, 1 nose piece of shell, 1 Hun shell case, also a few letters and papers which I found in a deep dugout which I explored. Their dugouts are very deep but smell horribly and the bedding looked very dirty. They must have left in an awful hurry, the rifle was still hanging up in the dugout.

'All the villages are pretty badly smashed up. I was disappointed in not seeing any dead Huns although I saw plenty of horses; my hat they did niff. It was jolly funny; we were driving up a road towards some crossroads. The road to the left went east and the one to the right went west. We stopped at the crossroads and started to argue which way to go. I didn't know where the line exactly was, but I knew that a wood which looked quite close was in Hunland. Some people were in favour of going east till they saw some Huns and suddenly there was a BANG, then a W-H-I-ZZ and then CRASH! just over our heads. One perfectly good burst of Hun shrapnel. I can tell you that it didn't take us long to go to the right. We came across a Hun tank which had been hit by a direct hit. Their tanks look more clumsy than ours but better to see where you're going. We drove home in state with a tender full of trophies.

'Archie is pretty good nowadays. I got a burst just underneath me this morning and found I was hit in two places when I got back. One piece through the tail plane and another through a rib in the plane. We went on a balloon "strafe" yesterday; it's rather good sport, but pretty exciting. We didn't shoot any down, but we made them pull their balloons down pretty quickly. I saw one of ours going down in flames; it looks very pretty from the air, but I don't suppose the old bloke in the basket thought so. The "balloonautics" always jump when they think they're going to be shot down, and generally they get down all right . . .

'PS I never took up Pelmanism. I found it cost £4 and the result at the end of the course was too vague. I think it would be more good to a businessman or somebody that has to remember things; we have to try and forget them as much as possible.'

On 26 September, the day the final Allied offensive was launched, Kirkpatrick's Squadron took part in a raid on an enemy aerodrome eleven miles inside Hunland. It appears as a fairly routine operation in the official communique: 'Several hangars were set on fire. A hostile machine was destroyed on the ground and 7 others were shot down. Five of our machines are missing.' But for Kirkpatrick it was the most hair-raising experience of the war and the only time he had a presentiment of death.

Just before the raid he wrote, phlegmatically as ever, what he imagined might be his last letter to his parents: 'If I live to tell you how I spent the hours from noon to 2 pm I'm sure they will be exciting. If I don't then you have the satisfaction of knowing that at least I was prepared for anything. Some people might blame me for putting the wind up you like this, but I think it's much better that you should expect the worst and then be bucked as anything if I do have the luck to get through. You remember what happened to Stone, I'm sure his people didn't expect it, and it must have come as an awful shock.'

In the event he was writing again, at 4 pm: 'I told you that from 12 to 2 would be pretty exciting but I had no idea that I would have the excitement that I did have and yet be able to write and tell you about it. I can't tell you what the job was but this is partly what happened. We all broke up the formation and dived on the objectives. I dropped my bombs on something which I thought would appreciate them, then I started charging about 100 ft up firing my guns at things on the ground till they wouldn't fire any more. Then I decided to come home. The Archie was awful, also machine-gun fire on the ground. I was trying to climb up at some of our machines which were going west, when suddenly there was a bang and my engine stopped.

'Imagine my feelings at the thought of landing about half a mile from where we'd been doing the damage. However, I picked a field and was just going to land when I thought I'd try my gravity petrol tank and see if by any chance I could get my engine to start. Fortunately it did, but I hadn't half the power that I would have done if my pressure had been working. Well, I decided to try and get home. I had about 11 miles to go till I got to our lines and there were no more of our machines in sight, so I decided my only hope was to come along so near to the ground that Archie wouldn't be able to see me so well, so along I came as best I could.

'My engine wasn't going very well and the wind was against me. You should have seen the expressions on peoples' faces. I went over a sunken road and saw 2 fat old Huns walking calmly along with their hands in their pockets; they simply stared at me with their mouths open. Then I saw 2 Fokkers up above diving at me. I simply tore round trees and churches with them firing at me. After what seemed years I saw some trees which I thought I knew were on our side, the machine-gun fire got very fierce suddenly, then stopped. I looked over and saw some Scotchmen waving to me Oh! SOME relief believe me . . .

'PS I found on landing that I had a bullet through my tank, the petrol was pouring out.'

As the British divisions stormed through the Hindenburg Line defences during the next few days, Kirkpatrick was engaged in a number of fierce dog-fights and ran the gauntlet of withering fire from the ground in low-level attacks on the retreating Germans. Extracts from two letters point up his comment that 'things are rather too exciting now'.

'We had a great scrap this afternoon. We met about 20 Fokkers and got rather involved with them. I stuck to Titch the whole time like a leech and saw Fokkers and Camels hairing round in a terrific muddle. I did a loop more or less by accident and found a Fokker going down below me so I went down and had a poop at him and then pulled away and chased my tail for a bit and in a few seconds there wasn't a Fokker to be seen. They suddenly appeared above us, miles above us, and we were at 16,000 ft, and after we'd been chasing round for bit they came down, at least some of them did, and then the noise up-started. Everything happens so quickly that I don't know quite how everything happened, still we all got back and I think we got 2 Huns for certain and 2 doubtfuls . . .'

'. . . The machine-gun fire from the ground is pretty awful. You see the old Huns crouching in the trenches and they "crack-crack-crack" away at you for all they're worth. Then the sight of our Tommies relieves you and you know you're out of Hunland. The line changes so quickly now, you can't tell beforehand exactly when you'll be in Hunland. Even when you get over on our side it's quite exciting with field guns going off underneath and shells bursting all round. One seemed to burst right under me this morning, I got an awful surprise.

'When we've dropped our bombs we career about the battlefield. It's awfully interesting and I really enjoy it. You see all sorts of things; burnt out tanks, Huns hanging up to dry in barbed wire etc. The best of it is, you can't smell anything...'

By the time Kirkpatrick returned from another leave with his family on 19 October, Izel le Hameau had been left far behind and the squadron was billeted in a village from which the Germans had been driven only ten days before. From the peace and plenty of that sylvan retreat, he was brought face to face at last with what war could entail in terms of human suffering. Until now a village in Hunland had been no more than a landmark from which to take a bearing in his cockpit, anonymous as a clump of trees or a river bridge. Now he rubbed shoulders with the reality. Because of his knowledge of French he acted as interpreter for the liberated villagers, and the stories they had to tell served to harden his heart against the idea of an armistice now being talked about. 'I'm full out to smash the Huns as much as possible' was the bellicose note on which he entered the final phase of the war.

'*30 October* . . . The civvies have got absolutely nothing, the Huns took away every blooming thing and, of course, there are no civvy trains running up here. We scrounge around and get bully beef and tinned things for the people in our billet for which they are very thankful. They are the most miserable crowd of people I've ever struck, and you can't wonder considering they've had the Huns with them for 4 years. The way they have been bullied the whole time is awful. The Huns used to go round the houses and requisition anything they wanted like clothes or furniture. The civvies had to pay awful prices for food, 40 francs for a pound of butter. They used to have to steal vegetables out of their own fields.

'They say that our prisoners were absolutely starved and

156

used to hunt round rubbish heaps for rotten food. The Huns were always fining them and taxing them too. They had to pay 50 marks to keep a little toy dog. The Hun soldiers seem to be very badly fed, which is good news. One loaf of black bread to last 2 days and soup twice a day was all they had. Most of their clothes are made of paper. The different branches of the Hun army hate each other apparently. The only person they really like is the Kaiser and him they worship. Apparently until a short time ago they thought they were going to win the war, they used to say that by next Spring they would be in London. They hate the British or "Tommy" as they call us. They say if it wasn't for us the war would be over, only we don't want to make peace. The civvies in Germany are very hard up for food. When the soldiers used to get leave they didn't go home because it was "trop triste". They used to go on the bust in Belgium where they could have a good time apparently.

'One sad thing about these people is that they have nothing to do or to look forward to. They just sit in front of the fire all day and mope and say that for them it's "tout fini". Now of course is the time when they hear that they've lost relations in the war. The other day the two inhabitants of this house, an old lady and a moderately young one, spent the whole day wailing and gnashing their teeth because they'd heard that the old lady's son had died of typhoid in the French Navy in 1915.

'An interesting thing is what they say about the French farmers. They used to sell their stuff to the Huns for a reasonable price, but the civvies had to pay an awful price for anything. The farmers used to prefer seeing the poor people starve rather than help them. These people say the farmers were just as much their enemies as the Huns . . .

'The things they tell us about the goings on of the Hun officers and some of the "ladies" here are simply extraordinary. I simply howl with laughter. The funny part is to hear old ladies of 60 telling you these things. If my letters didn't have such a wide circulation I would tell you some funny stories.

157

Take this one. The Hun kommandant got fed up with his wife, so he undressed her and made her run round a room with nothing on while he whipped her! You should hear our Madam talking about the Hun nurses they had here, "grossières debauchées" etc etc.'

Although the Allies had been deliberating for some weeks on the terms of the armistice requested by Germany, there was no let up in the fighting. Offensive patrols were now over a front so fluctuating that it was often difficult to tell which was Hunland. But in the air there was no mistaking the enemy. Kirkpatrick records packs of 40 or more, usually manoeuvring to lure the British fighters over to their side. 'Every time we go up we meet those blooming Huns' he writes on 3 November.

Kirkpatrick's last two letters of the war are no different in tone from the rest. They indicate how much war had become a way of life and how little prepared he was for the implications of peace. His letter written on armistice day echoes the sense of disbelief, even of anti-climax recorded in many other first-hand accounts. Except amongst the liberated civilians, there was no jubilation at the front. It was in England that the flags waved, the bonfires and fireworks erupted.

'*10 November* . . . Villages which were supposed to be in Hunland were full of cheering civvies, so we went east till somebody fired a machine-gun at us. We couldn't see anybody of course but we shot the village up just for luck. Then shortly afterwards we thought we were on our side of the lines and we came across a cart driving along a road. The soldiers just looked up at us, so we went on without taking any notice of them. When we came back we found that we'd been miles over and they must have been Huns. I did feel mad, specially as my guns were going so well that morning . . .'

'*11 November*. Rumour has it that this blinking war's over, supposed to stop at 11 am this morning. I'm blowed if I know whether to believe it or not. Anyway we've got orders to do our patrols a mile this side of the lines which is rather nice. Now we want to know what we're going to do. I expect that as the Hun evacuates Belgium we'll follow up and do sort of police patrols to see that they clear out all right. The CO says he expects we'll be moving at least once a fortnight for some time. I expect they'll be all sorts of funny jobs about now, and I expect it'll be awfully interesting.

'All the military bands in the place are playing. I lost 5 francs —I bet 5–1 that there wouldn't be an armistice, but I don't mind paying more than that for the blooming war to stop. I'm fed up though that we didn't shoot at those guys in the vegetable wagon.'

On his study mantelpiece at Wimborne Minster, where Yvone Kirkpatrick, OBE, TD, lives in busily contented retirement with his wife, squats a model of a Sopwith Camel made for him by one of the legion of public school boys to whom, over the years, he has taught German and French, a love of music and (as commanding officer of Canford's Combined Cadet Force during the last war) the rudiments of warfare. It is as difficult to equate that toy-like model with one of the deadliest machines in the air over France in World War I as to discern in this benign, burly, white-haired Mr Chips the lineaments of the trigger-happy young fighter pilot of 1918.

But to Kirkpatrick, the orchard and hutments of Izel le Hameau, the camaraderie of the Mess, the hedge-hopping and dog-fights over Hunland, are still close. His oldest and closest friend today was his Flight Commander in those unforgettable days—the 'Titch' to whom he 'clung like a leech' during that great scrap when he saw 'Fokkers and Camels haring round in a terrific muddle' and the Squadron chalked up '2 Huns for certain and 2 doubtful'.

'I was one of the lucky ones' he muses. 'And I know I have enjoyed life the more because I have never ceased to be grateful that, against all the odds, I survived.'

7 Besieged in Kut

The five months' long siege of Kut in Mesopotamia, which ended on 29 April 1916 with 12,000 emaciated British and Indian troops being herded across the desert to a barbarous captivity under the Turks which only the toughest were to survive, is one of the grimmest episodes in British military history.

To the public at the time the surrender of Kut, so soon after the evacuation of Gallipoli, was seen as a humiliating blow to British prestige. The disasters of Gallipoli and Kut were, indeed, the first indications to the peoples of the Middle and Far East that the hitherto all-powerful Raj was not infallible, and, as such, signalled the beginning of the end for the British Empire.

When reports reached home of ragged starving columns of British soldiers stumbling along under the whips and rifle-butts of their Turkish and Arab guards, of mobs jeering them through the streets of Baghdad, of their inhuman treatment in the Turkish prison camps, a public outcry led to the setting-up of a special commission. But by the time its findings were published, Kut had been largely forgotten—a minor incident in a remote sideshow to the 'real' war on the Western Front.

A number of books have been written about the siege (the longest in our history) and its terrible aftermath, ranging from eye-witness accounts to historical reconstructions seeking to

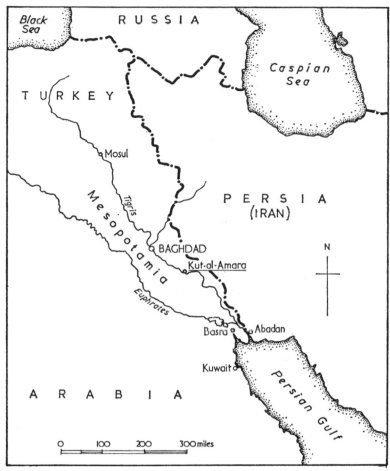

Mesopotamia, showing the position of Kut

apportion blame for a calamity that should never have been allowed to happen. But how many today could guess at the whereabouts of Mesopotamia (the modern Iraq) let alone Kut?

The fortress town of Kut-al-Amara, a squalid huddle of mud hovels in a wide loop of the Tigris some 250 river-miles south of Baghdad, sounds real enough in the letters written during the

161

siege by Captain J. S. S. ('Ian') Martin to his mother in Scotland as the besieged garrison awaited, with ever-dwindling confidence, the arrival of a relief force to rout the encircling Turks and put an end to the slow slaughter by shellfire and snipers' bullets and the tightening grip of hunger.

On 1 April 1916 Martin, an Indian Army surgeon aged 27, writes: 'Today completes the 120th day of the siege. This brings us level with Ladysmith, and fulfills one ambition of our siege enthusiasts. The men are beginning to weaken—nay, have weakened—so greatly that they with difficulty can carry their rifles and equipment the distance between the front-line trenches and their town billets.'

For reasons unknown he concluded the sequence of letters that day, with four weeks of the siege still to go. 'You will find this letter sent you in eleven separate covers, each envelope numbered and each page too,' he writes on the fifty-eighth and last page. 'I have taken this precaution against loss or censorship, and perhaps one or two may avoid both.'

The letters, which reached his mother intact, might never have come to light but for a 'shot in the dark' by Mr Roderick Suddaby, head of the Department of Documents at the Imperial War Museum. Early in 1974 with the help of Major-General H. H. Rich, CB, who had been a young infantry officer during the siege, he contacted the fifteen survivors of a Kut association that for many years had kept memories alive at annual reunion dinners in London. Among the names was that of Major-General J. S. S. Martin.

An entry in *Who's Who*, briefly recording his army career (mostly in India) up to his retirement in 1945, provided his address, a 5,000 acre estate on the Isle of Skye. But it was his widow who replied, enclosing the unique batch of letters. The General had died a few weeks earlier, at the age of eighty-five.

Mrs Martin recalls that when her husband's Kut letters were found among his mother's effects after her death and passed on to him, he showed little interest and did not even bother to re-

read them. He was a forward-looking man, she explains, with a great zest for life, living very much in the present. She was fifteen years younger than he when they married in 1924 and he had rarely talked about his First War experiences. One of the few Kut anecdotes she could recall was connected with its aftermath, when the officers were separated by the Turks from the rank and file and they went their separate ways to prison camps in Turkey, the former being treated with reasonable respect, the latter with a callous brutality only equalled by the Japanese in World War II.

'At one stage my husband must have been in contact with some of those poor other rank prisoners on the march,' says Mrs Martin 'for he mentioned having given his spare pair of boots to a soldier whose feet were in a terrible state and next day seeing him barter them with a guard for a few cigarettes.'

That Martin, for all his grounding in the rank-conscious traditions of an Indian regiment, saw his mission as relieving suffering wherever he found it is apparent from references in his letters to his surreptitious tending of starving Turkish prisoners and his care for Arab townspeople wounded during the siege. But only rarely does he hint at the gulf that separated officers and other ranks even in the extremity of a siege. 'It is difficult for us officers to realise their hunger and weakness' he writes a month before the surrender, by which time men had been driven to supplement their near-starvation rations with the meat of cats, dogs, hedgehogs, starlings, sparrows. 'We officers have all the time had at any rate a sufficiency of palatable food and enough Mess stores to give a change of diet when needed.'

From what he confided after retirement to his son-in-law, it seems clear that the letters (written, as he indicates, with the censor very much in mind) tell only half the story of Kut and that his reluctance to re-read them might have been partly because he was acutely aware of the fact.

'He spoke to me perhaps more openly than he would have

done to people closer to him, and was very bitter about the whole business of Kut' says Dr M. B. S. Cooper, a St Albans general practitioner married to the elder of Major-General Martin's two daughters. 'He felt the staff officers had "chickened out", isolating themselves in their mess, and that the other ranks had been badly let down. He said that all the books written about Kut had covered up the awful behaviour of the officers but that he could never bring himself to write about it with survivors still alive.'

Mrs Martin describes her late husband, who was the son of a Gaelic-speaking Scottish Free Church minister and an Irish mother, as a man with a 'tremendously strong nature who could have put up with a very great deal before cracking', a dedicated army man with a great gift for organisation, but one who 'never did anything from a sense of duty, always from a sense of interest or amusement'. To such qualities one may add an overriding sense of compassion in reading the letters he wrote as he laboured to save life with death so close around. Although towards the end he admits that 'the pleasures I once had in writing of this cursed siege has very completely evaporated', it is a mostly buoyant account he gives of what it was like to be cooped up week after week 'in hourly peril of one's life—by bomb, shell, disease, most dangerous of all, the sniper's bullet', to thrill to the distant 'sounds off' of a relief force's artillery only to have hope dashed by news that they had 'dismally failed' to break through, even to mark as a red-letter day the discovery of a forgotten tin of peppermint toffee after two sugarless months.

It was basically to protect the Royal Navy's oil supply in the Persian Gulf that an expeditionary force of the Indian Army launched the campaign in Mesopotamia with the capture of Basra in November 1914. Sun-scorched and insect-infested in the hot season, a flooded morass in the cold, its featureless wastes were dubbed 'the land of Sweet FA with a river running up it'. But for the brief spotlight on Kut, it was a 'forgotten army' of half a million men who fought there until final victory near the end of the war, and who left 30,000 dead behind.

The siege was the outcome of a rash attempt to capture Baghdad by a division of the expeditionary force under Major-General Charles Townshend, and it is this action which Martin describes in the opening of his first letter (written three weeks after the siege has begun but in evident expectation that his mother would soon be in receipt of it).

'You will know before this reaches you how our army marched to Ctesiphon, 15 miles from Baghdad, where they defeated the Turks who were holding a very strong entrenched position. Our troops stormed the place at night with the bayonet, took it, and held it in spite of counter attack after attack—five times they came on again before desisting. Our losses were enormous—roughly five thousand out of the twelve that went into action. Then the Turks produced two new divisions and we had nothing for it but retire, as we were seven thousand to their fifteen–twenty thousand. Of course they had lost enormously at the battle, but scarcely more than we.'

Martin was already stationed at Kut and he was appointed Medical Embarkation Officer with the task of arranging for the carrying ashore of the mostly untended wounded from the over-crowded vessels that had brought them from the battle area, feeding them and sending them on to the small general hospital in Kut to be dressed and 'classified'. The more seriously wounded were then reloaded on to deeper draught vessels for the long trip to Basra.

The hopeless inadequacy of the medical arrangements is implicit in Martin's account of the '8 dreadful days' when 4,609 wounded passed through his hands, not counting Turks. 'Among the little tasks I had was the purely voluntary one of feeding, dressing and clothing about fifty wounded Turks. I contrived to do this with the aid of my sub-assistant surgeon on

L

the quiet: as my OC Major Baines would have been very annoyed if he found me doing anything but "evacuating". If I had done nothing they would have gone to Basra undressed and unfed. They were starving, poor things. I raided the bakery at 11 pm the first night and by all sorts of dodges and excuses managed to get them hot bread, ½ loaf each, which they simply wolfed, bad cases and all equally ravenous. Next day I ranged the bazaar with an interpreter and bought up what dates and bread I could find—and could pay for as it came out of my own pocket—and so rationed them fairly well before sending them down river. The Turk is very patient and enduring of pain and hardship: the men didn't grumble or whine though their wounds were often ghastly—a pleasant contrast to the often behaviour of the Indian patient.'

When the Turks finally closed the ring around Kut on 7 December 1915, the already densely packed Arab population of 6,000 had been swelled by 10,000 British and Indian fighting men, 3,500 Indian non-combatants and some 2,000 sick and wounded. Formerly the centre of a busy grain trade, Kut boasted a mosque, a flourmill, two bazaars and a scattering of two-storey houses and gardens, but was mostly a maze of alleyways flanked by mud hovels with matting roofs, filthy and insanitary beyond description. In a small village on the right bank of the Tigris opposite was a woolpress and a liquorice factory. Surrounded by desert, it could scarcely have been a more dismal and unsavoury setting for a siege, and the complete lack of foresight by the expeditionary force's high command is indicated by the fact that provision has been made for only 100 hospital beds for British sick and wounded, 325 for Indian.

Martin's account of the siege begins as the last stragglers of the field army were arriving after their exhausting retreat from Ctesiphon, often running the gauntlet of enemy fire (the letters were mostly written some time after the events described and dates have been given only when relevant).

'Our quiet village of Kut has now entirely changed. Horses,

tents, sick, guns all over the place: gardens trampled flat: roads driven through walls, houses and orchards. Everywhere litter and untidiness: the arriving force had no thought but to put up a shelter, cook a mouthful of food, and go to sleep. Mule carts were unhitched anywhere and the drivers went to sleep under the carts, generally leaving the unfortunate mules to fend for themselves. They had marched forty miles the last day with the enemy at their heels.

'Next day everyone was scratching holes in the ground. We who had stayed in Kut found it difficult to believe in the imminence of the enemy's attack. No 4 Field Ambulance hadn't heard a shot fired in anger since the few shells in April at Alwaz. However, as we saw everyone else digging in we followed their example in a somewhat feeble fashion. Anyway, we dug some deep trenches for our own British sick—about 20 in number. I had about 200 Indian sick in my section but couldn't hope to tackle shelter trenches for such a number. My sick also were about $\frac{1}{4}$ mile away in a very thick orchard and I hoped would be well out of shell fire.

'The main ambulance camp and our mess were on the fringe of an orchard and most of the tents were in the open. But the danger to us here arose from the presence of one of our own batteries about 100 yards in front, and some heavy guns on our right. The General Hospitals formed an enormous camp to our right and being right in the open must have been plainly visible to the enemy, as the sick were either in big marquee tents or in reed huts.

'On the 6th December the Cavalry Brigade marched out with most of the transport and the Horse Artillery. The enemy began to shell us that afternoon and made things most unpleasant in our camp. Our artillery replying, the enemy's fire is directed to the battery just in front of us and in consequence we get a large number of the shells intended for our guns. We had now a big shelter made of hay bales about 2 layers thick erected, in which we established a dressing station. But we have no place to keep the wounded, who after being dressed have to lie in the open in the tents. Luckily no one is hit.

'This day we make the acquaintance of "Windy Lizzie" a long-range howitzer mounted on a barge. Her little gift is a 5 inch leaden shell full of high explosive. She gives a little distant cough and after some time you hear a high-up whistling noise which seems to get nearer, nearer, louder and more menacing, followed by a tremendous bang, or about equally a soft plop, for her shells don't always go off. Mostly you don't hear the preliminary cough: the first warning is the whistling, then you listen for the bang and wonder where it will be. She is rather erratic in distance and you can never be certain what she's aiming at: but one of her efforts is sure to land somewhere near you in the end. She is the worst of the lot as you can't get any cover worth while from her shells, which seem to drop vertically from the blue.

'The other characteristic Turkish gun is the little quick-firing mountain variety. A battery of four pops off, about 6 each gun —pop pop pop bang bang bang—without a pause for five minutes or so and the air is simply full of noise and smoke of bursting shrapnel. But these are easy to avoid if you sit tight in your funk hole or dodge behind a palm tree. Of course the Turks have got lots of ordinary field guns—one hears an estimate of eighty guns, and they help to keep things lively.

'Anyway the General Hospitals found things getting a bit too hot for them and so they decided to move into billets in the town. This they did on the night of the 7th. To make room for them the whole bazaar was turned out and each little shop became a tiny ward in the new hospital, holding about four patients. The bazaar consists of rows and rows of such shops on each side of a central roofed-in roadway. We started moving in about 5 pm and finished stowing away the sick by 5 am next morning. I suppose there were about 600 to move. So now if you wander through the bazaar, not eastern wares, but wounded men are on show; it is really one of the queerest sights in the world.

'We ourselves stuck out the 8th in the open, without casualties: trying to dig ourselves and our sick in as best we could. The morning of the 9th I had detailed a party to work on a new dugout, and gone off to get roofing stuff from the engineers. When I returned I found two of the party had been killed and three wounded and that the men were a bit fed up: especially the patients who couldn't move from their tents. When our OC heard of the casualties he went straight off to the General, and got orders to move into billets in town at once. After a bit of searching we found the billets in which we are now quartered, gave summary notice to quit to the Arab owners, and moved in the same evening, sick and all.

'Our mess house is a typical good class Arab quarter. Downstairs three dark rooms open from the square courtyard. Two are used by our British personnel, one by us as mess. Very dark and cold they are as the only light comes through the door. Upstairs it is very pleasant. On one side is a long well-lighted room with plastered walls and carpeted roof and floor. In this we three junior officers live and very comfortable we are too. Opposite us is the OC's bedroom—about half the size of this. Round the inside overhanging the courtyard runs a verandah: and over the verandah and courtyard spread the fronds of two great palms.

'Two similar houses serve for British Hospital and Assistant Surgeons and are facing us on the other side of the street. The Indian hospital is adjacent the Mess in two blocks. Indeed when we first arrived the sick and wounded very soon filled up both blocks and we founded a "convalescent home" in a disused Turkish bath about ¼ mile away where all the slightly wounded go, coming every day for medicine and dressing here. This Turkish Bath or "Hamam" is the quaintest place I think ever utilised as a hospital. It is almost underground and very dark. The big room is lined by couches which do excellently for the sick and the central circular room, which has a furnace underneath, is hot and moist and does very well for chest cases.

169

It is a bit damp as water is of course laid on all over the place: but it's very warm and comfy and so deep down that it were miraculous if a shell pierced it.

'On the 10th the enemy made their first infantry attack, coming in at night and entrenching about 600 yards from our front line . . . We took and held the "Woolpress" village on the right bank on the 10th, as enemy snipers were giving us a lot of trouble, and we have kept it since. The bridgehead on the far bank of the bridge of boats, put up for the marching out of the Cavalry Brigade on the 6th, was held by a small detachment but the enemy, fearing our use of the bridge either to attack them or as a means of retreat, attacked the holding party in force and captured the bridgehead. We had then to recapture the bridge with a strong force and to avoid further trouble blew up the far end resting on the right bank, so that the whole thing drifted on to our, left, bank, and has there remained since. This affair cost us a good many casualties as some of the more severely wounded had to be abandoned on the right bank: but the Turkish general was very courteous afterwards and sent in twice to let us know how our wounded men were progressing!

'On the 12th and 13th they made attacks en masse on our front which failed dismally. So they stopped attacking for a bit and spent their time sapping up to us. So that by the 17th they were up against our barbed wire entanglements and beginning to sap under these. Both sides now used bombs freely, and all houses were raided for mirror glass for periscopes. The night of the 17th we made a sortie from the fort and captured 30 or 40, killing a lot more. After that they were more careful and a later sortie was scarcely a success, as our men found the invaded trenches empty and they were heavily enfiladed on their way back. The enemy again attacked in force on the 20th, lost very heavily and retired.

'But their big attack was on the 24th. It began in the afternoon with a really heavy bombardment of the town, also of the fort. They knocked out one of the two guns in the fort and did a lot of damage to the wall. In the town a lot of houses were hit. Our British Hospital was hit—the body of the 4 inch shrapnel embedding itself in the outer wall: the nose passed through the shuttered window, killed our store sergeant and also a sick sergeant just below the window. Three more inmates were wounded, and altogether we were rather annoyed, as this was the first shell that had done us any damage.

'That night the enemy brought up two field guns to within 200 yards of the fort and simply blew in the whole front, burying the defenders. They then rushed it with bombs and carried and held the NE Bastion. We bombed them out: they got in again: finally they found it too hot and retired leaving some 50–60 prisoners and about 1,000 dead. These attacks sound very curious from our billets. Usually one hears only the crack crack of our own and enemy snipers: then perhaps you hear it develop into a slow rattle with the birr of our maxims and the tut-tut-tut of their machine-guns plainly audible. Every now and then a bullet sings past or phuts against the wall. But listen to the rattle deepen to a steady roar which seems to come in great waves of sound—every now and again a big boom! of a bomb or a field gun: and the air even here, 1 mile away, is fairly alive with singing bullets and you duck behind the wall as you rush along the verandah to the bedroom.

'Then next morning the wounded begin to come in—or more often next evening, as it is too exposed to move sick by day. Then we in the ambulance have fairly got to set to— digging out bullets: setting fractures: opening and cleaning up wounds: tying bleeding vessels—work for all and lots of it. So we lie awake of nights listening to the roar of musketry and wondering how much work we'll get next day!

'Then it's not very easy to be as calm and collected as one would like when going about one's work during the day. For up to the 24th they kept buzzing shells at us all day and most of the night too. And though by God's mercy only one of the lot hit our hospital still all round us shells were bursting and people from the houses all round came in wounded and many men were killed. Many of the local Arabs suffered. There have been days when every single house round us had its quota of killed and wounded, and we unscathed. Our walls would not help to stop the shells: they have not done so in other houses: it was simply God's mercy for the poor wounded and sick.

'These bullets I have mentioned as singing by are the cause of a good many casualties. We have had five or six such among our patients—none serious however. They must needs be very spent before they can drop into our courtyard. One of my best bearers was shot through the chest while having a look round from a rooftop. Another was hit in the forehead—he has been operated on and will live—while bringing in a wounded officer. Otherwise personnel unscathed.

'The enemy have snipers on the other bank who practice shooting down all the streets running at right angles to the river. It is pitiful to see the poor Arab women rushing down at nightfall to fill their waterjugs. One or two of them are always brought to hospital wounded. We have become the favourite hospital for the Arabs. I had some success in digging out bullets from various inaccessible places: and our fame has spread abroad. Moreover, we put "Medicine" on their wounds: other ambulances not so—they put the dressing on straight away. They come all ages and sexes—pretty little girls with bullets in the groin to hoary old sinners with shrapnel in the belly. They do make marvellous recoveries—and as a result we try rather marvellous operations on them—so far invariably successfully. So that our street is full of Arab seekers-after-health every day.

'Though we have had but few patients injured by bombard-ment it is very different with the General Hospitals. They are nearer the river front, and so to our heavy guns, which attract the enemy's fire. They cover an enormous area of the town. Every day fifteen to twenty shells hit them somewhere: the marvel, is not that they have casualties, but that any survive. I myself one day saw a shell land on the roadway and kill two and wound one sepoy about 20 yards away. I was able to give first aid—luckily as the man was bleeding very freely. But it's not what you expect in a hospital. And just about five yards away Barber, the OC of the hospital, was calmly sewing away inside a bullet-smitten abdomen, with two doctors assisting him.

'Another day, looking in at the Stationary Hospital operating theatre, King, of our service, was cutting off the remnants of a leg. "Hullo," I said, "who's that you're amusing yourself with?" "Oh, only one of my sub-assistant surgeons" was his answer. "He got his leg blown off and two orderlies were killed just in the office about twenty minutes ago!"

'As the enemy trenches have closed in, so the wounds from our front-line trenches have become more severe. They are often inflicted at point-blank range and the wound is consequently "explosive"—ie a comparatively small wound is seen where the bullet has entered but the exit is a great bulging mass of torn muscles, tendons and crushed up splinters of bone. All you can do is to give an anaesthetic and cut away the protruding mass and clean up things as best you can, hoping that it won't go too awfully septic. Of course in trench warfare a very large number of the total wounds are through the head: these only come into the ambulance to die: one can do absolutely nothing for them: they are already unconscious and need no anodyne.

'For myself I got laid up with influenza on the 24th and it certainly doesn't tend to bring your temperature down to have these beastly shells banging and screaming about: especially when people are killed not five yards from where you are lying in bed and practically in front of your eyes. However, Xmas day by some unspoken contract was kept in absolute peace and rest. Not a single shot was fired the whole twenty-four hours: even the snipers ceased. They say it was partly due to the German advisers of the Turkish C-in-C. The Turks also wished to collect and bury their dead at the Fort—which I understand they were permitted to do.

'Our Mess gave a sort of Xmas dinner party. We tried our best for a long time previously to get a goose or even a pair of ducks for the feast: but these, cheap and easily obtained in normal times, were quite unprocurable. In the end we were content with a couple of fine fowls which cost us 6/8d the pair. They were plump and tender, but in normal circs would be dear at 8d each. So with other things—eggs are now 2d each, instead of 4d the dozen. Still I don't suppose in Edinburgh 2/- a dozen would seem very exorbitant for fresh eggs—and these are really big and milk fresh. We are lucky in having a cow which gives us about a quart of milk daily. We can't expect more as fodder is scarce. This cow is a windfall from No 1 Field Ambulance, which, having lost all its equipment in the retreat, had gone down river to refit.

'Our ambulance ponies are in rather a dangerous spot—not far from where our old camp used to be. Three horses have already been killed, three more are in the veterinary hospital. The latter include my poor old Sanvar, who after being wounded slightly was finally bowled over on 3rd January by a bullet in the shoulder. Today I hear he is developing tetanus and the vet shakes his head over his chances. Poor old fellow, he was far and away the most delightful pony to ride one could imagine and certainly the hardiest polo pony that ever chased a ball. However, I shall not lose money over him as he is not now worth his purchase price of £50, which was what I gave for him. Government, you see, compensates you on the basis of purchase price. It seems funny now to think that I once owned £200 worth of horseflesh, and now have none at all!'

That within a matter of weeks the term 'horseflesh' would have taken on a more urgent, utilitarian meaning was evidently far from Martin's thoughts when he wrote the above. 'All the talk now is of the relief,' he writes on 8 January, 'when it arrives, when it starts, where it starts from, of what strength is the relieving force—and so on.' Even though it was known that some 20,000 Turks stood between them and a relief force, surrender was never really envisaged until early in April.

On 21 January, in a deluge of rain, lashed by an icy wind, the first relief force, under General Aylmer, was defeated in the Battle of Hanna. To the besieged garrison, as Martin indicates, it was the more frustrating to have their would-be liberators within earshot. 'On the morning of the 19th and the whole night previously the ground of Kut reverberated with the incessant rumble of the relieving force's guns, twenty-five miles distant: as light grew the horizon was white with the bursting shrapnel and the smoke of the enemy's return fire. In our trenches they say you could hear quite plainly the sharper rattle of rifle fire.

'The noise of the guns gradually became an occasional thud instead of a continuous boom, the shrapnel clouds became individual, and then finally ceased to be seen: and we hoped that the ridge had been taken, and that we should shortly see the enemy columns filing past.

'We did see one such column, and a joyful communique to the garrison announced that the first of the Turkish retreat had begun: but we now believe to our sorrow that it was a convoy of wounded, and with not a few of our sepoys as prisoners. For the attack had dismally failed: the first-line trenches were carried and the order was to hold them at all costs: but a fierce counter attack with bombs drove back all but the Black Watch, who held on alone till their remnants were practically wiped out. So we in Kut, disappointed and disheartened, settled down to enjoy the prospect of a prolonged siege as best we might.'

A communique from General Townshend stating that he had 'ample food for eighty-four days', though he confidently expected to be relieved 'in the first half of the month of February', brought cold comfort to his troops, the colder because they were now suffering the deluge that had bogged down the relief force, with added refinements of discomfort.

'The streets became long lakes of muddy water—I got wet above the knees one evening returning from an afternoon's bridge with the Flying Corps. Our hospital compound became too dreadful at this time: there is of course no system of drainage and such means as we could use—big pits etc—were of little avail as they soon flooded over. The cesspits which each house has in plenty also overflowed with an indescribable odour. Many of our wards leaked heavily and in one the mud roof partially collapsed over our patients.

'Meantime imagine the state of affairs in the trenches. The floor of these had been by this time trodden hard and the clay had become quite impervious to water. So that every drop stayed where it fell: in time the communication trenches became so full that, in spite of hostile fire, everyone had to move over the open. Then pity the poor wounded, soaked to the skin, numb with wet and cold! Coming in to a hospital which could not give them a dry shelter and only in direst need an extra blanket or change of clothing. We always managed to dress their wounds and clean them up a bit, and give them a hot drink and morphia if necessary.

'The rains kept on for nearly a week: the nights became steadily colder and soon several degrees of frost were nightly registered. The rains in the hills had swollen the river, which was rising a foot every day. Finally on the wettest night of all the sepoys' misery culminated. The river one night overflowed its banks and burst in a great wave, first into the Turk trenches —which were about fifty to 100 yards in front of ours—and thence into our front line through the Turkish saps. We managed to dam it back long enough to turn our maxims on to the retreating enemy for the Turks had to run too—and then it was a case of every one making a rush for our second-line trenches about 300 yards back. We lost a few men by rifle fire but our machine-guns literally mowed down the enemy, who had no communication trenches at all, and who refused to retire quicker than at a walk.

'These rains proved a perfect godsend to the garrison. The enemy were forced to retire right back to the sandhills about two miles away. Their second- and third-line trenches were equally flooded. They had now not even a picquet in touch with us. You can picture the relief of our fellows now able to walk about in perfect freedom in the open: no enemy within sight: not even a sniper in range. Only a couple of days before the enemy all round them, their sapheads right under our barbed wire and in places less than thirty yards away: the crack of rifles incessant: bombs and trench mortars banging everywhere: and the final attack imminent any moment. The rains compelled us to evacuate our front-line trenches for about half a mile, but this only strengthened our field of fire, and when the water went down strong picquets were posted in the old front line.

'About this time the fuel question was very serious. The men were getting only a handful of brushwood with which to cook their food. Luckily the abandoned Turkish trenches were simply full of wood and the delighted sepoys lit huge bonfires everywhere and dried their clothes and blankets with great cheerfulness. We sent out some raiding parties to the sand hills and captured a few prisoners—but annoyed the Turks who retaliated by sending picquets and snipers close in: so that the reign of absolute peace came to an end abruptly and our fellows had to keep carefully behind their own wire and under cover once more. But the Turkish sapheads and mine galleries were gone for good and with them all fear of successful attack by assault.'

With the failure of the first relief attempt and the prospect of a prolonged siege, food became the crucial issue. Until then the garrison had been on a full ration or more and it was later suggested that there might have been a very different outcome to the siege had General Townshend made a thorough assessment of all available supplies at the outset and started distributing them on a scientific basis. He was also criticised for making no provision for the fact that most of the Indian troops were forbidden by their faith to eat meat. Without an alternative to the horsemeat that now became the mainstay for the British troops, hundreds of them fell prey to sickness and disease, adding to the problems of the already overtaxed medical staff. It was only near the end of the siege that near-starvation, coupled with a threat by Townshend to demote those who still stuck to their religious scruples, drove them to accept the forbidden flesh.

What the rank and file, both British and Indian, must have suffered as they grew visibly more emaciated can only be guessed at between the lines of Martin's letters. He writes about how the officers fared, on a comparatively varied diet that to the Tommy and Sepoy must have seemed little short of prodigal, but even so can describe himself at one stage as having 'never been so consistently and chronically hungry in my life before'. But at least, unlike those officers he was later to condemn as having 'chickened-out', he shows himself aware of the much greater plight of the other ranks.

Martin's first reference to rationing comes late in January when 'the question of relief faded into the background and, as in all sieges, *food* became the dominant question. We carefully went over our Mess stores and calculated how long they would last. The Commissariat announced a revised scale of rations. Bread was lowered to 12 ounces daily: jam and butter were issued in small amounts to make up: bacon stopped: tea was very much reduced. Paraffin oil ran out altogether as all oil had to be reserved for the grain crushing mills. Petrol was cornered for the same purpose.

'Now if we go over the advantages of Kut in a siege the chief is that it is normally a great trading centre for the surrounding agricultural country, and a favourite trade route from the Persian highlands. The whole of the export trade of corn was stopped by order of the Governor of Kut early in November. So great stores of wheat and barley—mostly the latter—had accumulated here when our retreating division arrived. Now you will see the reason for the grain-crushing engines, and the saving of the paraffin. Very soon the entire stock of ordinary flour ran out and we became dependent on the three oil engines we were lucky enough to find installed here. A mixture of about one part wheat to four parts barley flour now is used in making our bread, and is issued to the Indians to make chupatties. This makes the most delicious bread you ever tasted: one knows it is made direct from the pure grain: nothing is wasted—it is dark brown and delightfully flavoured . . .

'Sugar gave out almost at once, also molasses for the Indians. Milk—well, we stuck to our cows as long as we could: but one cow and her calf soon succumbed to the necessity for a meat ration. We were on bully beef for quite a while: then they began to slaughter the draught oxen of the heavy 5″ guns. Luckily we had about 120 of these, the finest bullocks in India and such beef! As the Indians weren't getting any they did us quite a long time.

'About three weeks ago (early February) the first horse fell under the butcher's knife. Since then they have been slain daily, about 20 at a time. About 2,000 mules and 3,000 horses and ponies have been cooped up along with us: we kept them as long as we might but as they each eat daily about ten men's grain ration you can see that they are a considerable burden on the community. So we began on them as soon as we could, before the bully beef or the bullocks were quite finished. For a long time officers' messes generally got a bit of beef if they wished but now are reconciled to daily horse. We have him in steak and kidney pie, horse olives, horse mince, horse rissoles, potted horse, horse soup, stuffed horse heart, horse liver etc ad nauseum.

'The other staple in our ration is the date. I expect you have by this time received the dates I sent you before Xmas. Well do you know, I have many a time in this siege been selfish enough to wish I had kept that case for myself! It must be the weather, or the brown bread, or the muchness of work that does it, but I have never been so consistently and chronically hungry in all my life before. I had quite a good lunch at 1 pm and already am longing for four o'clock tea though I have an hour to wait. To return to our dates—he turns up every day in our ration— 2 oz each—and we have him for pudding at dinner in various disguises. He is excellent by himself with a dash of ginger and lime juice, and a little boiled rice to tone him down served with him. He makes an excellent and savoury mush stewed with a few dried apricots: date charlotte is delicious: date dumpling is a dream: and he is an excellent ingredient of suet puddings.'

On 22 February there was a second abortive attempt to relieve Kut. General Aylmer's artillery shelled the entrenched Turks at Hanna for twelve consecutive hours, but failed to dislodge them. In Kut the troops had been alerted to take the offensive at any sign of a Turkish retreat.

'Immense excitement prevailed in Kut as our GOC Townshend had been promising us early relief and we had known for some time that something was brewing. Here we had to organise our bearer sections and get transport etc ready to move out against the enemy should they be seen to retire. We actually knew nothing about it till five am on the morning of the attack when the Major came in with a lamp and told us to be ready to move out to our positions in the front line trenches by seven am. What a scurry and rush to get boxes and haversacks ready, waterbottles filled, emergency and ordinary rations issued. Of course we were wild with excitement and expectancy. From our roof we could see the whole sky west of us lit up by glaring flashes and the air was filled with the incessant distant booming of the guns. Alas our hopes! We returned sorrowfully to our billets that evening—to learn next day that the whole attack had been abortive—that nothing more than the artillery duel we had heard had taken place.

'So we settled down again to routine, and locked up our boxes and became a little more despondent as to our ultimate chances. Also we began to hunt round with even greater energy for any foodstuffs that might still be available on purchase—with only moderate success. The usual routine began—breakfast at 8.30—surgical cases till twelve—lunch at 1—operations at 2—tea at 4—exercise in the shape of walking round to various Messes and exchanging views as to date of next attempt at relief, rumours as to numbers of relief force, river floods etc, an occasional game of bridge.

'About this time enemy aircraft made their debut at Kut. We were very interested one morning in a curious monoplane—dark in colour, with what looked like squares—really Maltese Crosses—on the wings, but didn't really take much notice of the thing, as our own planes were coming over us every day and no one thought of the Turks having such a thing. However, that same evening the beastly thing came again, and we were startled by a series of tremendous explosions, some of them very near our ambulance—quite unlike our old friend Windy Lizzie's shells—much louder—earth-shaking—clouds of black smoke and debris hurled hundreds of yards. The annoying part of it was that these were our own bombs abandoned during the retreat.

'Next day there was a great buzz taking precautions against more bombs. We mounted six anti-aircraft guns and one of the 13-pounder horseguns was tilted up and fixed on a swivel. So that when the old Fritz came along, flying low, as usual, he got the surprise of his life when the whole lot blazed off at him—nearly got him too. We got fairly used to Fritz in time. He used to roll up nearly every evening and drop about six bombs at a time—sometimes making several trips back for more.

'We believe—up to the present it has never really been proved—that a double roof protects from aerial bombs—ie the bomb hitting the roof bursts in the room immediately below, but leaves unharmed people on the ground floor. Our new house is two storey and we have put a layer of tents on the floor just above the mess which we hope will help to keep out bombs—

but of course we would rather no experiments were tried. I personally have so far had no very narrow escapes from air bombs, but one fell into our hospital compound when I was out and nearly got our two majors and the PMO who was inspecting the hospital at the time. Luckily Major Bennet saw the bombs dropping and they all ran for shelter, else they had been pulverised. It tore a great hole in the ground about 5 feet deep by 8 across. We made use of it by extending it a little, roofing it over, and running off waste water into it as a huge soak pit.

'One bomb, a hundred-pounder, fell on an Arab house just beside our mess, and completely demolished it, burying fourteen people under the ruins. Of these two were taken out alive but terribly shattered—and in spite of what I could do for them both succumbed very soon. Another hundred-pounder was dropped one evening when Fritz came over just before dark—it fell into the British General Hospital and, hitting the thin roof, went off just below spreading out and killing and wounding thirty-three Tommies—of whom eleven were killed outright and two later died after operation. I believe our General has since sent a protest to the Turkish commander about this "outrage". Certainly the last few times he seems to have carefully avoided the vicinity of the hospitals. As a matter of fact, owing to the way in which guns, supply stores, hospitals, headquarters etc are mixed up in the centre of the town it would be almost impossible to avoid hitting the hospitals if you aimed at —say—the arsenal.

'We have all a very wholesome respect for Fritz, who usually comes alone, but has on occasion brought one or more friends with him. We much prefer to be strafed by Windy Lizzie though she is a much more numerous genus. He has twice come over at midnight making a most fiendish row, for he flew very low—and giving us all such a scare with his beastly bombs that we left our bedrooms upstairs for the rest of the night and tried unsuccessfully to finish our sleep on the cold hard floor of the mess, where at all events we were comparatively safe. You can't imagine what a tremendous noise an aeroplane engine can make on a dead calm night when it's just 1,000 feet or less over your head.'

On 8 March the garrison was again keyed up for a break-through by the relief force, this time in an assault on the Turkish reserve force entrenched behind the Dujaila redoubt, a vast earthworks on the right bank of the Tigris some five miles from Kut.

'The long-expected day arrived, and we got out our boxes again, summoned and equipped our sections, and proceeded to our new positions in the trenches. The garrison was ready to sortie at a moment's notice. We were going to cross the river by a bridge below the town and attack the Turkish right flank in rear, while Aylmer stormed it in front. The whole of the operation centred on the attack on the Dujaila redoubt. If this were carried, the enemy's flank was turned and his communications with his main camp above Kut cut off below the River Hai: also by our guns we could command the enemy's bridge of boats over the Tigris connecting their forces on both banks.

'Well we had a most exciting morning: the roar of guns was continuous the whole of the morning of the 8th, and we could hear them coming ever nearer and could see innumerable shrapnel and lyddite bursts on the horizon. We know now our people were scarcely five miles from us: we were all discussing what we should have for our relief dinner, and what time of day we thought Aylmer would arrive. But the roar of guns continued steadily, and we heard great crackling bursts of rifle fire. Still no movement among the Turks, no signs of the expected retirement.

'All day and through the night the bombardment continued, next day too—till about noon when all became quiet again. Then we heard—Aylmer sent a communique and our General published his wires to us, with a long screed of his own too. Our relief force had stormed the redoubt and been thrust back: they could get no water, for they were five miles south of the river, and in the end had retired, losing some 2–3,000 casualties. Townshend's letter to his troops pointed out clearly our new and dangerous position and asked us to hope on and fight on to the bitter end.

'The immediate consequences of the defeat in Kut were a decrease in the rations and a wholesale destruction of horses and transport animals which were left. A few are still kept for butcher meat but the entire grain supply had now to be reserved for the garrison. As our paraffin supply became low, the mills became unable to cope with the amount of grain requiring milling. A large amount of the grain ration had therefore to be issued untreated—simply unhusked, and we had to do our best with this to turn it into food. So if you look in to our hospital yard you may see any fine morning about twenty bearers hammering, grinding, sifting the grain. The product is made into a kind of gruel which is served to—and heartily detested by—the patients.

'All local produce was long ago commandeered for the hospitals—eggs, milk, chickens etc. We still, however (29/3/16) are carrying on with tinned milk, and butter and jam nearly ad lib. We shared out all the mess stores in equal portions. Each member of the mess is at liberty to fix his own date for relief and proportion his mess supplies accordingly. For instance I have four tins of jam, two of milk, and 5/6 lb of butter to last me to the end. I am counting on this arriving in about sixteen days—certainly no more. So one tin of jam lasts me 4 days, but a tin of milk must do 8 days! It's jolly difficult in this warm weather. Our OC however is reckoning on 21 days and has to eke his stuff out in proportion. I may be left in the lurch but what matter? I shall have lived luxuriously for a time, anyhow.

'We aren't doing so badly now—7.30 am tea—breakfast 8.30 bowl of porridge, fried fresh fish, rice (ad lib) bread butter and jam, tea coffee or chocolate with milk and saccharine—lunch 1 pm tinned salmon, tinned pineapple, bread and jam, coffee—tea 4.30 pm oatcakes, bread and jam—dinner, clear soup, fresh fish, steak and kidney pudding, stewed dates and rice, liver or sardine on toast. I am not any thinner, I assure you. I suppose you must have gathered from this long letter how very largely the food question has bulked in our view of life! Indeed it is with some pride that No 4 Field Ambulance mess can compare their catering with the majority of other peoples' . . .

'Well, mater mine, if this letter should ever finish it will I hope be to describe the relief of Kut and the joyful scenes we can anticipate therewith. I am still a prey to grave doubts as to the probability—nay the possibility of this ever coming. Even should it come I may not be there to greet our relievers. For here one is in hourly peril of one's life—by bomb, shell, disease or, most dangerous of all, the sniper's bullet. I was standing in my bedroom doorway the other morning when a bullet splashed into the wall above my head: every time I move outside my room I am in danger from the stray bullets which are constantly whistling—thank heaven mostly overhead.

'*1 April 1916.* I was surely in melancholy mood when I stopped writing the above. But we mostly are bored and fed up: and the pleasure I once had in writing of this cursed siege has very completely evaporated. I want to get it up to date, though, and it certainly passes the time fairly well. Also I do hope that you have been keeping up the weekly letter in the hope that it will soon be getting through to me: and I can't tell you how much I am looking forward to reading them all. One does envy the generals who get their weekly mails regularly by aeroplane. There have been a few favoured individuals who have also had their letters occasionally—mostly staff officers and hangers-on. Feeling is very bitter just now on the subject: it is difficult to see for what reason certain officers have been able to get their mails sent them and the regimental people in particular, none of whom have been so favoured, are specially bitter.

'The aeroplanes now come every day and drop various articles—bank notes to pay for local labour and food stuffs have been one of the principal freights. They come in wads of half a lakh of rupees: the light bundle they make is very difficult to drop accurately and rumour hath it that at least one lot was blown by a strong wind into the enemy's lines. Saccharine, Dover's Powder, anti-tetanus serum, millstones, compound squill pills, cigarettes, buffer springs for guns, rifle pull-throughs, flypapers(!) are only a few of the miscellanea of our requirements so sent. The saccharine is one of the greatest boons to my mind—all British troops were made a free issue and so was ended one of the chief miseries of the siege for your sweet-toothed son—he had sugar, or something like it, in his tea once more.

'Today completes the 120th day of the siege. This brings us level with Ladysmith . . . The only ration now is—British $\frac{1}{2}$ lb bread, 1 lb horsemeat: Indian 10 oz barley flour (of the crudest description, largely chaff) only. They [the men] wish the siege ended and care not which way so they get their bellies filled. It is difficult for us officers to realise their hunger and weakness— we have all the time had at any rate a sufficiency of palatable food and enough Mess stores to give a change of diet when needed.

'I am now going to bring this letter to a close. I hope I have succeeded in interesting you and helping you to realise this rather marvellous siege. I am afraid that as my interest in events declined, so failed my descriptive powers. Possibly I have provided but a dull ending.

'I don't think I have yet told you how the discovery of the siege was some toffee you got some lady to send me from England. Peppermint. I had one tin left which I had forgotten. The discovery was historic. It was at the end of February, when none of us had tasted sugar for two months. By jove how good it was!

'Then one eventful day I opened, at long last, my box of shirts. I had been saving them up for just such an emergency as we are now in. The wounded were without any available change of clothing—they came in soaking wet and chilled to the bone from the trenches. Now the shirts weren't very warm, but they were clean and white and with blankets and hot bottles were really delicious to the wounded. They are really beautifully made—I feel as if I should love to wear them myself!

'If relief should come, I hope to write to let you know all about it but this letter will at any rate let you know that it has come. I may find myself too busy to write at any length, as there will be all the sick and wounded to evacuate. Even should the worst happen, and we fall into the enemy's hands, I hope to plead the Geneva convention and to get away before the end of the war. The Turks have certainly so far tried, I think, to observe the convention, and certainly have shown themselves (as our Intelligence proves) humane and considerate in their treatment of such prisoners as they have captured . . .

'Goodbye then, darling mother. I have been longing for news of you and also specially of Jim, the family soldier . . . Au revoir—your loving devoted son, Ian.'

Four weeks later, on 29 April, a flutter of white flags over the British lines signalled the surrender of Kut. As a last desperate attempt to keep going until relief could be achieved, the air-drop of supplies from the few primitive aircraft available (the first operation of its kind ever attempted) had merely prolonged the siege for a few more days. When the garrison was reduced to their two days' emergency supplies Townshend had no option but to capitulate.

Since the commencement of the siege, 1,746 troops had been killed or died of disease. But for the Tommies and the Sepoys the real agony had only begun. The inhuman treatment to which they were subjected in captivity was to cause the deaths of 1,700 of the 2,592 British other ranks, 1,300 of the 9,300 Indian. The Turk was to lose any of the grudging respect he may have earned at Gallipoli or during the siege itself as horrifying reports reached home: of the stumbling columns of prisoners, parched and starving, blinded by sun and dust, herded by whips across the desert: of stragglers left to die from exposure under the blazing sun or to have their throats cut by scavenging Arabs: of stinking overcrowded prison camps where cholera and dysentery took their toll unchecked: of young British soldiers forced to submit to the homosexual demands of some of their captors.

It was scarcely surprising that Townshend, acclaimed at the time as the 'hero of Kut', found himself shunned when he returned to England after the war. He had lived in luxury throughout his captivity, an honoured 'guest' of the Turks, and had done nothing to intermediate on behalf of the troops he had professed (in one of his last communiques) to love 'with a depth of feeling I have never known in my life before'.

For his officers (some 220 British and 200 Indian) there was a 600 mile march into Turkey after the initial five-day voyage by paddle-steamer from Kut to Baghdad, but gruelling though this was their treatment by the Turks was as 'humane and considerate' as Martin had envisaged. Boredom was their chief enemy as they languished in prison camps for the rest of the war.

Mrs Martin recalls her husband mentioning that he learned Turkish while a prisoner ('though he had no use for the Turks at all') and that the fortnightly parcels sent by his mother never reached him—he later learned they had been appropriated by another officer called Martin at a base camp. But for her this part of her husband's life before she knew him is shadowy. The man she talks about is the 'very dedicated army man', brilliant but unambitious, who reached the peak of his career in World War II when the organisational ability he had shown at Kut came into full play as he supervised the medical services for 60,000 wounded troops flooding out of Burma: the father of their four children, brought up by her in Scotland and a bit in awe of him when he returned after his retirement in 1944: the kilted Scottish laird of the estate entailed to him in Skye, where, after so many years of enforced separation, they came closer in later life than ever before.

'My father-in-law was a very impressive man, powerfully built, every inch the retired General,' says Dr Cooper. 'At first sight he might seem a typical "pukka" Indian Army General, until you noticed the twinkling friendly eyes. He was a very fine doctor, a great historian, knowledgeable about all sorts of things and with enormous intellectual depth, an astonishing man. We don't breed them like that any more.'

There is one last glimpse of him in those far-off, half-forgotten days when the struggle for survival was all, in a letter he wrote to a lady he had befriended on his first voyage to India to join his regiment and who had subsequently passed it on to his mother. The first seven pages of the letter were written on 1 April 1916. 'It is an occupation rather suited to All Fool's Day to sit down to write letters when it is by no means certain that the said epistles will ever leave Kut—except on the person of the writer and, like himself, in durance vile, en route to Baghdad' he starts, and goes on to give a résumé of 'the four months of our investment which are in retrospect like the troubled night of a fevered sleeper'.

The eighth, and last, page was written nearly four months later, presumably at a temporary halt nearing the end of the long trek to the final prison camp. Martin writes in the back of beyond, one among millions of individuals caught up in the strange happenings of war, but momentarily spotlit, alive because here he happened to jot something down, whether from an urge to communicate or just for something to do to pass the time to the next happening. What that was cannot be known. The picture fades into the darkness from which it emerges.

'*15th July 1916.* The forebodings in the opening page of this letter have proved too horribly true. Here I am, after much journeying and many tribulations, sitting in my blanket shelter at ? a camp whose name I forget—about 3 days' march from Ras-al-Ain which is the southern terminus of the still incomplete Baghdad–Aleppo railway. At my feet runs a little muddy stream almost dry—around and upon my feet are myriads of insects—mostly biting flies, but including some thousands of ants, great and small—houseflies, big horseflies, and several unknown and noxious small species. Overhead the Eastern Sun, smiting me through my thin blankets—which are disposed upon sticks about six inches above my head.

'I eat weird oriental food, cooked in a fashion by my Indian orderly. But you must excuse me, for a gust has blown my shelter down. I shall resume another day. Meanwhile goodbye my dear friend—yours affectionately, Ian.'

Acknowledgements

I am greatly indebted to the Imperial War Museum for access to their archives and for permission to reproduce some of the illustrations used in this book. In particular I would like to thank Mr Roderick Suddaby, Head of the Department of Documents, for his expert assistance in selecting material and assessing its significance in the context of history.

A Place Called Armageddon would not have been possible to compile without the support and encouragement of the Editor of *The Sunday Times*, Mr Harold Evans, and grateful thanks are also due to Mr Derrik Mercer, News Editor.

Finally I would like to thank Mr R. C. Case and Mr Yvone Kirkpatrick for the illuminating commentaries they provided on their youthful letters, and to the relatives of Guardsman H. G. Boorer, Midshipman G. L. Drewry, VC, Captain G. W. Nightingale and Major-General J. S. S. Martin for supplying valuable background material.

M. M.